D0245739

Keys to Engagement

**Review of Care for People with
Severe Mental Illness who are
Hard to Engage with Services**

ISBN: 1 870480 36 8

Published by

The Sainsbury Centre for Mental Health
134-138 Borough High Street
London
SE1 1LB

0171 403 8790

RC Royal College of
OT Occupational Therapists

WITHDRAWN

0 0 0 0 2 2 0 3

Contents

Foreword

Care for severely mentally ill people has made major strides forward in the last thirty years. A range of innovative and effective mental health services has been developed within local communities. However, services remain patchy and some service users continue to receive an inadequate and uncoordinated response to their needs.

Unfortunately, it is often those patients who are most vulnerable who receive the least appropriate care. Some find it difficult to engage with existing services but sometimes hard pressed services reject or exclude needy individuals rather than actively persevering in working with them.

People with severe mental illness who are difficult to engage seem to be at greatest risk in this regard, yet if this group is not receiving the care they need the consequences can be grave. It was an appreciation of the urgency to develop a range of local services for this group which led me to commission this review from The Sainsbury Centre for Mental Health.

The Review clearly identifies the range of services which can deliver high quality, effective and safe care to this client group. Particular attention needs to be paid to the provision of assertive outreach teams, accommodation with support, and daytime activities and occupation. Delivering such care in the right way may cost society no more, and conceivably less, than providing inadequate care.

I should like to thank the Review team for all their hard work, and to congratulate those services which are already providing high quality care for this client group. I would strongly urge the relevant policy-makers, commissioners and providers of services to implement its recommendations. There is a small transitional cost to restructuring the services to make them more effective, but the consequences of not responding will be continued social exclusion for the group itself, and further damage to public confidence in mental health services as a whole.

Lord Sainsbury of Turville

Acknowledgements

The Steering Group for the Review is listed in **Appendix 2**.

In addition, The Sainsbury Centre for Mental Health would like to thank:

Lead editor:

Dr Emma Seymour
(Consultant)

The Sainsbury Centre for Mental Health:

Dr Richard Ford
(Head of Service Evaluation)

Steve Morgan
(Training & Development Officer)

Dr Paul O'Halloran
(Head of Training)

Sue Parkman
(Researcher)

Dr Diana Rose
(Senior Researcher)

Dr Geraldine Strathdee
(Head of Service Development)

Dr Judith Wolf
(Head of Research)

Consultants to the Review:

Tahera Aanchawan
(Consultant)

Professor Max Birchwood
(Service Director, Early Intervention Service, North Birmingham Mental Health Trust)

Dr Alan Cohen
(General Practitioner)

Yvonne Christie
(Consultant)

Dr Adrian Grounds
(Senior Lecturer, Institute of Criminology, Cambridge University)

Dr Sonia Johnson
(Senior Lecturer, Department of Psychiatry & Behavioural Sciences, University College London)

Dr Parimala Moodley
(Consultant Psychiatrist, Pathfinder Mental Health Services Trust)

Professor James Raftery
(Professor of Health Economics, University of Birmingham)

Service-users:

Les Bailey
(User Group, The Sainsbury Centre for Mental Health)

Bill Downer
(User Consultant)

All those who participated in the interviews

Carer:

David Posnett

Services visited for the Review:

Nottingham Rehabilitation & Community Care Services, Nottingham Healthcare Trust

Mental Health Services of Salford NHS Trust

The Elmore Community Support Team, Oxford

Thames Reach Housing Association, London

Thanks also go to all those who responded to the call for evidence placed in the *Health Service Journal* and *Community Care*.

Executive summary

The purpose and scope of the Review

There is a small but significant group of severely mentally ill people who have multiple, long-term needs and who cannot or do not wish to engage with services. Unless engagement is achieved and people in the group are provided with safe and effective services, they will continue to face social exclusion. Public confidence in services is determined partly by the adequacy of services for this group.

This Review has focused on the needs and aspirations of people who are not engaging with services and has examined how services can best address those needs. It has developed a core service model and a series of steps which need to be taken nationally and locally to enable systematic service development across the various agencies involved.

The audience

This report is aimed at all those who have a commitment or duty to meet the needs of this client group, including central Government, the NHS, local Government, the independent sector, providers of housing and employment schemes and others. The findings will be of interest to staff working in services which have, or should have, contact with the client group, and to service users and their carers and advocates.

The structure of the Review

In developing a strategy to meet the needs of the client group the Review aimed to:

▷ define the group, estimate its size, and describe the main needs;

▷ outline a core service model which can meet those needs;

▷ examine current policy, practice, research evidence, and specific service models, to determine strengths and weaknesses;

▷ develop a practical strategy to move current services forward.

In working on this report, the Review team received information from a range of service providers and undertook site visits and information gathering exercises with support from The Sainsbury Centre for Mental Health. The Review was chaired by Dr Matt Muijen and led by a steering group representing key stakeholders.

The context

It is estimated that the client group for this Review consists of about 15,000 people nationally, who are concentrated in deprived areas, often in inner cities. Most have never lived in the old mental hospitals, but may have experienced repeated inpatient stays, coupled with sometimes unsatisfactory community placements. Some will have histories of offending and others will be homeless. Many will have a history of substance misuse or self-harm; some will be a risk to others. Most experience poor social functioning, stigma and isolation.

Why does the group not engage?

Individuals within the group fail to engage with services for a variety of reasons, some due to individual experience or characteristics, others due to the inappropriate nature of services. Many are suspicious of statutory services because of their upbringing, life experiences or attitudes. They may feel that services have little to offer or may have experienced negative staff attitudes, including racism. Services may find it difficult to engage because they are too focused on immediate outcomes or on medical treatment alone, or because they lack the staff with the appropriate skills and the time or resources to achieve engagement.

What are the needs of service-users?

The generic needs of users in this client group differ little from people with severe mental illness generally. They embrace adequate income, accommodation, daytime activity and health and social care including support with daily living and specialist mental health interventions. However, they have a specific need for engagement, practical support and intensive contact to allow them to access services across a range of agencies. Many also need ready access to specialist support in areas such as substance misuse and offending.

What are the gaps in current policy and provision?

Policy and provision have not been constructed around the needs of this group for a variety of reasons. A number of strands of recent policy and service development have been helpful but current services for the group are fragmented, and there is a lack of direction from the centre about what should be provided where. The importance of 24 hour nursed care has been emphasised. While this is a vital service component, it is not clear that it is an effective solution for the group as a whole. It is also a very expensive option.

The international evidence supports the establishment of an assertive outreach function, delivered through assertive outreach teams where the client-base is large enough, but this has only been implemented in a minority of the areas which have a significant population of the group. The possible value of assertive outreach is supported by an illustrative economic analysis which shows that a revolving door style of management or 24 hour nursed care are both less likely to be cost-effective than a combination of assertive outreach and supported housing.

The Review team visited, and collected evidence from, a number of services which are engaging with the group using a variety of models including assertive outreach (or intensive case management), 24 hour nursed care and intensively supported ordinary housing.

The conclusions of the Review

In areas where there are significant numbers of people from this client group, it will be difficult, if not impossible, to meet their needs through generic community mental health teams. Assertive outreach is required to engage and maintain engagement with clients and this requires considerable staff time and effort. Assertive outreach can usually best be delivered through teams of health professionals and outreach workers to ensure the right mix of day-to-day engagement and active healthcare and rehabilitation. Where the client-base is too small to justify separate teams, alternative models are proposed, including having selected individuals within the community mental health team who specialise in working with this group.

Staff delivering assertive outreach need to:

▷ have the right skills, background and attitudes;

▷ be properly supervised and managed;

▷ receive appropriate training and support.

Without these characteristics and inputs they are unlikely to be able to work in a way which will engage those in need of care. The style of working by staff is key to engagement - they must be able to go out and meet people on their terms, in their normal environment. They must also be able to persist in this approach over considerable periods of time.

Assertive outreach alone is not enough. Staff must be able to provide a range of services within the team and access other services across a wide group of agencies. In order to achieve this it will be necessary for the relevant agencies locally to come together to prepare and implement a specific plan for the group. The task for the staff and agencies involved is to tackle the social exclusion of this client group. Unless this is done it will be difficult to achieve positive outcomes in either health or social functioning.

The Review underpins this analysis with six key findings supporting 15 recommendations.

The six key findings

1 **There must be a strategic approach to the needs of the client group both nationally and locally**

> Each Health Authority should set up an inter-agency strategy group to plan and monitor provision for the group (*Recommendation 1*). Its first tasks will be to establish a local definition of the group, to commission a needs assessment, to benchmark local services, and to develop a plan for services.

2 **Assertive outreach is the core function required from mental health services in relation to the client group**

> All Health Authorities with a sufficient client-base (i.e. 100-150 people) should create one or more assertive outreach teams to take the lead in engaging with the client group (*Recommendation 2*). Where the client-base is too small to justify this, other appropriate arrangements should be made to deliver the assertive outreach function.

3 **A human resource plan is required to enable the implementation of assertive outreach**

> The lead agencies should agree a set of core criteria for the selection of staff to work with the client group (*Recommendation 3*) based on those suggested by this Review. Teams will require a range of expertise so that individual team members can act as resources for the team as a whole (*Recommendation 4*). Training strategies must also be developed and implemented (*Recommendation 5*).

4 **Teams must be effectively managed**

> Managers of front-line staff must be visible to staff and accountable for service delivery (*Recommendation 6*). Team members must have protected caseloads of around 10-15 clients (*Recommendation 7*).

5 **Teams must develop a style of working which matches the needs of the clients**

> The Review identified a range of characteristics which should be present in the teams. Services should make every effort to maintain contact with the families of clients (*Recommendation 8*). Suitable arrangements need to be put in place for cover that is available 24 hours per day, 7 days per week (*Recommendation 9*). Local strategies and service delivery must reflect the needs of black and ethnic minority populations (*Recommendation 10*).

6 **A range of provision for teams to draw upon must be available across the relevant agencies**

> Teams providing services for the client group should negotiate service level agreements with partner agencies (*Recommendation 11*). A sufficient supply of suitable supported accommodation (*Recommendation 12*) and a range of daytime activities including employment opportunities (*Recommendation 13*) are required in each planning area. Clear arrangements for accessing safe 24 hour care, including inpatient care, (*Recommendation 14*) are vital. Finally, mechanisms for liaison with local child and adolescent mental health services are required to allow early intervention (*Recommendation 15*).

CHAPTER 1

The client group for the Review

This chapter:

▷ **explains the need for a review of care for people with severe mental illness who are difficult to engage with services;**

▷ **describes the process of the Review;**

▷ **estimates the size of the group.**

1.1 The need for a review of care for people with severe mental illness who are difficult to engage with services

This Review arose from the urgent need to focus attention on a small but significant group of people with severe and enduring mental illness who find difficulty in engaging with services. All of these people experience major and constant personal suffering and disabilities as a consequence of their illness, but some of them also present significant challenges to services and to society in general.

The client group for the Review

This Review addresses the problems and care of people with severe and enduring mental illness. Many of the people in this group have complex and multiple needs but share two key features:

▷ needing long-term and intensive support;

▷ being difficult to engage or having difficulty in engaging with services.

For the purposes of this Review we have adopted the following definitions:

▷ **severe mental illness:** "a mental disorder (i.e. psychotic disorders including schizophrenia, manic depression or severe depression or severe neurotic conditions and personality disorders) of such intensity that it disables people, preventing them from functioning adequately as determined on the basis of their culture and background";

▷ **long-term:** "a period of at least 12 months, but often of many years";

▷ **intensive:** "a need for input at least on a weekly basis" .

The characteristics and needs of this group

Many of the people in this group, broadly known as "revolving door" patients, have repeated brief admissions to psychiatric beds. Some will have spent longer periods in the past as inpatients or are still occupying hospital beds, and are sometimes known as the "new long-stay". Others may be caught in a cycle of repeated offending. They may be homeless or have many changes of address. Many combine mental health problems with substance misuse problems. Some may have a history of violence against others; many more will be at risk of suicide, self-harm or severe self-neglect. Many members of the group will have experienced problems since adolescence and will have received care from child and adolescent mental health services. Some will have been under the care of social services. Very poor social functioning may make members of the group living in the community isolated and stigmatised. Many of these characteristics are illustrated by the case study in **Box 1**.

Box 1. Case study: Carl's story

Carl is 27 years old and lives alone in council accommodation, although he also spends a lot of time in his mother's flat, which she shares with one of his sisters. He left school at 15, not having gained any formal qualifications. He began training as an apprentice draughtsman and took football trials with a professional club.

At the age of 17 Carl was arrested and charged with assault. While being held on remand his behaviour was agitated and he was also suicidal. He claimed to be possessed by an evil spirit which told him to adopt a leadership position in the final war between good and evil. He was instructed to cleanse the world of the opposite forces, but he was confused as to which side he was on. He was assessed and given a diagnosis of schizophrenia.

The next 10 years have been characterised by repeated assaults causing actual bodily harm, arrests, detention under the Mental Health Act, and periods of probation. He considers his medication and any contact with the mental health services as harmful and is only sporadically compliant with treatment. He uses cannabis and considers that his family, the mental health services, the criminal justice system and wider society are "setting me up each time by making me take medication that does me harm, while society tries to stop me using the things that mellow me and chill me out".

He denies any need for mental health services and because he associates community staff with medication, he spends long periods of time avoiding contact. When he is in contact with his keyworker, he speaks intermittently of experiencing distressing suicidal ideas. However, he does not believe that the services can help him and takes the view that day centres can do nothing for him, because being with mentally ill people gives him no motivation.

Due to his chaotic and aggressive behaviour he has lost both his employment as an apprentice draughtsman and his football training opportunities.

The service response to the client group

It is clear that services are still struggling to develop an adequate range of care options for the group with which this Review is concerned. For example, several studies report that mental health services can fail to offer continuing care.[1,2] There is a particularly high risk of care breaking down after a hospital admission for men who are diagnosed as having a psychotic disorder, come from minority ethnic groups, live alone, and have been admitted under a section of the Mental Health Act. Sometimes users are discharged from hospital without aftercare services being in place despite a history of poor engagement and frequent breakdowns. At other times, staff report that they do not know how to engage with users who consistently refuse all services, despite considerable needs, risky behaviour and an inability to cope. It seems that the fit between mental health services and the people in greatest need of care is poor, and that staff and users are equally dissatisfied.

Many members of this client group are genuinely very difficult to work with and help. Some people might take the view that the services on offer are not appropriate, acceptable and accessible. Others, taking the reverse view, might argue that services are available to the client group which they wilfully refuse to accept. The Review did not adopt a position which would constitute an attack on either the service users or the people who plan, and work in, the services. There was instead a debate about why exactly it is that the client group and services fail to mutually engage, and why, if initial contact succeeds, treatment plans (including adherence to medication) so often collapse.

Rather than simply conclude that current services have failed to meet the needs of the client group, the Review looked at ways in which the style and mode of service delivery could be improved and targeted more precisely on the client group. This process included teasing out some of the ambiguities about the aims of services. Realistic expectations about the high levels of support that will be needed over many years are of particular importance. Some of the conventional divisions between acute or emergency care on the one hand, and rehabilitation and continuing care on the other, are also not helpful in planning services for this group. Many people in this group require a mixture of all these types of care at any one moment or repeatedly over time.

A test-case for mental health services

Although this report focuses on the difficult-to-engage client group, many of the issues raised here are of equal relevance to the wider population of people with severe mental illness. Successive reviews and inquiries have stressed the need to improve equity, quality and coordination of services if they are to function effectively for people with severe mental illness. This Review shares that position while also suggesting that the response to this hard-to-engage client group is a touchstone for mental health services as a whole. Public confidence in services will stand or fall according to their ability to adapt to the complex needs of this small but significant group.

The Review also took the position that the hard-to-engage group cannot be catered for solely within existing structures. Some distinct strategic changes in both policy and practice are required if this group's needs are to be met and their social exclusion prevented.

Pressure to provide more beds for the client group

An essential part of any service is the provision of a safe environment, usually in the form of hospital beds. However, a reflex response to problems in the community is to provide more beds, rather than expand community services. The current emphasis on developing 24 hour nursed care is analogous in some ways to the drive to develop medium secure provision for mentally disordered offenders. Although both these bricks-and-mortar solutions are necessary as part of the essential package of services, they also need to be judged on the basis of opportunity costs, including the complementary community services which may be foregone as a result. They are expensive strategies which require significant investment of capital and revenue. Too often, confinement is the final step in a long line of neglect and mutual misunderstanding, rather than a component of a comprehensive and flexible service. Equally, however, we have to recognise that insufficient provision of 24 hour nursed care and other high support accommodation has, in the past, put community services under sometimes intolerable pressures.

A high cost / low volume group

The direct costs of caring for people with severe and enduring mental illness are high. It has been estimated that the total direct cost of treating schizophrenia in the UK amounts to £397 million and the indirect cost to as much as £1.76 billion.[3] Cost is not evenly spread across all people diagnosed with schizophrenia. For example, it has been estimated that 10% of people who are treated for schizophrenia require long-term care in intensive community programmes or in 24 hour care settings. This 10% accounts for nearly 80% of the direct costs of mental hospital treatment and care for people with schizophrenia.[4] The cost of the group this Review addresses is disproportionately high, even within the 10%, as figures later in this report will show. This means that the cost-effectiveness of care for this group will have major consequences for the cost of mental health care as a whole.

Public safety and inquiries

A difficult question about this client group is raised by the issue of violence. For many people, thinking about this group of difficult-to-engage clients will raise memories of well-publicised incidents of violence which symbolise the failures of mental health care as a whole. Whether suicide or homicide, each incident is a major tragedy to victims, the perpetrator and staff alike. About 1000 suicides and 50 homicides a year involve people in contact with specialist mental health services.[5]

Some of the people committing such acts are part of this group, but many are not. Nevertheless, the lessons from inquiries are particularly relevant. Inquiries have repeatedly identified comparable problems in mental health care across the UK. These problems are all relevant to the care of the diffcult-to-engage group:

▷ lack of an identifiable responsible person or agency;

▷ fragmentation of care;

▷ poor risk assessment and management;

▷ under-resourcing of services.

Over-representation of black and minority ethnic clients in the group

A special question is raised by the over-representation of people from black and minority ethnic communities in this client group. The Review consulted with representatives of specialist mental health services working with minority communities, and with black service users, and there was extensive discussion of why mainstream services often seem unable to engage them.

Combating the social exclusion of people with severe mental illness

Other reviews and inquiries have stressed the need to involve a wide range of agencies and interests in designing and implementing mental health services. The present Review gave particular weight to these issues and this is reflected in the recommendations in **Chapter 7** of this report. Mental health services are dependent on the development of a range of accommodation options and the expansion of the opportunities for purposeful daytime activity for clients.

Even though mental health is central to an individual client's ability to cope, it was felt that services could not succeed without taking a much wider view of the group's problems. Many of the interventions do not concern a person's health so much as a cluster of social problems – housing, income, employment. Those interventions involve a wide range of agencies, including health, social services, housing, employment, social security, forensic psychiatry and education.

Social exclusion is one of the client group's central problems. Equally, one of the overarching goals of a strategy for the client group should be to work on all fronts to prevent such social exclusion. A key aim of services should therefore be to facilitate clients' access to mainstream facilities wherever possible. This makes it even more imperative that somebody takes the lead in coordinating a strategic response to these needs in order to avoid fragmentation and neglect.

1.2 The process of the Review

The Review was led by a Steering Group of external experts together with key individuals from within The Sainsbury Centre for Mental Health. The terms of reference for the Steering Group form **Appendix 1** to this report. Members of the Steering Group are listed in **Appendix 2.**

Research for the Review commenced in October 1996. In the first instance, a literature review was undertaken to define the characteristics of the client group. Desk-based research continued throughout the Review.

A limited programme of site visits and meetings with key organisations was undertaken between January and April 1997 by staff from The Sainsbury Centre. The Sainsbury Centre is grateful to David Posnett, a carer, who accompanied staff on some of the site visits. The programme of visits was planned using advice from within The Sainsbury Centre and from the Steering Group. In addition, a call for evidence was published in the *Health Service Journal* and *Community Care* in February 1997. This is reproduced in **Appendix 3.**

Views on the particular problems of service users from black and minority ethnic communities were sought by a variety of means, including a half-day focus group. Participants are listed in **Appendix 4.**

A few semi-structured interviews with members of the client group were conducted by a small group of user consultants to supplement existing Sainsbury Centre user research.

The Review also consulted with a number of experts who were not members of the Steering Group, and with colleagues within the Sainsbury Centre itself.

A variety of terms is used in the field to describe the client group and the problems of its members. The terms "patients", "clients" and "service users" can be used to describe individuals, and "severe and enduring mental illness", "severe mental health problems" and "mental distress" to describe their condition. This Review sought to avoid making a judgement on the correct terminology to describe members of the group, and so used a variety of the current terms.

1.3 The scale of the problem

People with severe mental illness who need long-term and intensive support but who are also difficult to engage, are a diverse group. This group is spread unequally across the country and receives inequitable care. Prevalence will vary considerably from area to area, related to contextual variables such as deprivation and the presence of, for example, railway stations and homeless hostels. Service factors such as the presence and high quality of a range of care options will lower the prevalence of hard-to-engage people. Finally, prevalence will depend on definitions used, such as the inclusion criteria of schizophrenia and the acceptance of people with severe personality disorders.

The proportion of people with severe mental illness included in the Review

Diagram 1 represents the prevalence of the Review client group by using a model of Russian dolls. The largest doll represents the group of people who present with mental health problems – about 10 -25% of the population annually, largely seen in primary care. Inside this fits the doll representing people with severe mental illness (2-4%). The group of people whose severe mental illness is also enduring fits inside this, and smaller still is the group this Review addresses.

Prevalence of severe and enduring mental illness

Some impression of prevalence can be gained from available figures. However, caution is necessary, since the methodology is rarely comparable and is also variable in quality.

It is particularly confusing that prevalence data often use different denominators. Some report rates for the general population; others for the adult population (age 18-65). Since the group at risk almost exclusively falls into the adult population, this is the more appropriate denominator, which we have used wherever possible. Many studies, however, only report general population figures. For those we converted these rates into adult population figures by adding 33% to the rates, the approximate proportion of the population under 18 and over 65 years of age. Since this is a crude approximation, we have also given the rates for the total population from which we derived the adult rates.

Some studies have attempted to identify all people with severe and enduring mental illness in an area. In Kensington, Chelsea and Westminster (KCW), a survey identified 1.2% of the adult population as falling into this category. 87% of these were in contact with mental health services. Just over 60% suffered from schizophrenia or another psychosis. Their prevalence rate is likely to be an underestimate, since people not known to any agency in this area could not be identified, and this could add as much as 50% to the percentage.[6]

In Camden, a point prevalence study of schizophrenia found a rate of about 0.77% in the North and 1.29% in the South where all the stations and homeless hostels are located (0.56% and 0.98% of the resident population).[7] Similarly, in Croydon a prevalence of psychosis of 0.5% was found, and in deprived Camberwell a prevalence of 0.9% (0.37% and 0.68% of the total population).[8] In contrast, in rural Nithsdale, a figure of 0.36% was reported (0.24% of the total population).[9]

DIAGRAM 1: ESTIMATING THE NUMBER OF PEOPLE WITH SEVERE MENTAL ILLNESS WHO ARE HARD TO ENGAGE WITH SERVICES

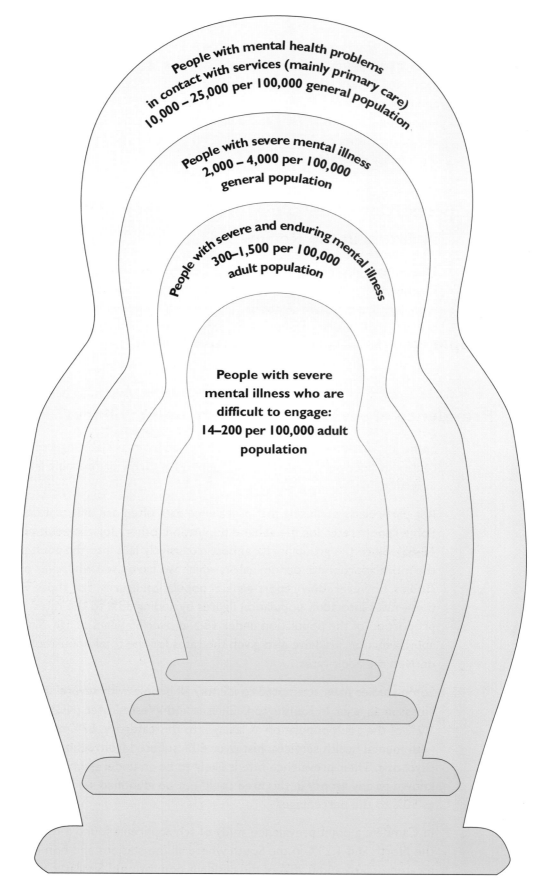

People with mental health problems in contact with services (mainly primary care) 10,000 – 25,000 per 100,000 general population

People with severe mental illness 2,000 – 4,000 per 100,000 general population

People with severe and enduring mental illness 300–1,500 per 100,000 adult population

People with severe mental illness who are difficult to engage: 14–200 per 100,000 adult population

(prevalence per 100,000 per year)

Most of these people need and accept intensive support. A needs assessment study in Bexley found that 75% of people with severe mental health problems in contact with specialist services had active clinical problems. 35% were deemed to be at risk, and of these 22% did not take prescribed medication.[10]

Over-representation of black and minority ethnic groups

In many studies a disproportionate number of people with severe and enduring mental illness come from an ethnic minority background. In KCW 25% of service users represent 12 different non-white groups, compared to 19% of the whole population. However, the Black Caribbean community is over-represented threefold. This high proportion of black users is typical of figures in many other reports. It applies to the comparative proportion of diagnosis of severe mental illness, hospital admission, section rates under the Mental Health Act, and occupation of secure beds.

Another complexity is the diversity of cultures from which people with severe mental illness come. In KCW, the total group speaks 56 different first languages. In Newham, almost 200 different faith communities with varied approaches to mental illness were identified.[11]

People who are homeless and mentally ill

Homelessness is a major problem for people with mental illness, and especially so for the highly vulnerable group this Review addresses. Becoming homeless can be a consequence of a client being difficult to engage and resistant to services, but may also be a result of services failing to achieve engagement.

Estimating the number of people who are homeless and mentally ill is problematic because of the difficulties with case definition, both of homelessness and mental illness. However, the most recent studies suggest that 30 – 50% of the homeless population who are in hostels, night shelters and on the street have some form of severe mental disorder, with severe mental illnesses such as schizophrenia predominating.[12]

Recent studies of people with severe mental illness in a given area (see above) have found that between 1.4% (Croydon) and 19% (Kensington, Chelsea and Westminster) of the group were homeless or in short-term accommodation. Many more have problems with their accommodation – for example, 20% in Bexley.

People with a dual diagnosis of severe mental illness and substance misuse

Substance misuse is a growing concern, and highly associated with the client group for this Review. A recent study in South London found that over one-third of all people who had a diagnosis of severe mental illness and who were in contact with mental health services also had a problem related to use of drugs or alcohol.[13] The most commonly used substances were alcohol and cannabis. In KCW, 10% of people with primary mental health problems were dependent on alcohol and 5% misused drugs. In Bexley this figure was 9%. However, all these figures are likely to be imprecise and are probably underestimates, since detection is largely subjective.

This problem has already been identified as deserving special attention in the US.[14] The characteristics of people suffering from severe mental illness and substance misuse are typical for this Review. As compared to people suffering from mental illness alone they are more often male, tend to be younger, are managing their lives poorly, show greater aggression and suicidal tendencies, have poorer medication adherence, and experience more frequent hospital admissions.[15]

People who combine dual diagnosis with homelessness

A recent report by the Homeless Alliance found a disturbing interaction between homelessness, mental illness and substance misuse.[16] Over 50% of people with mental illness surveyed in cold weather shelters misused drugs and/or alcohol. Most of this group had spent time in institutional settings. Moreover, 53% of those with homelessness and substance misuse had been sleeping rough for over five years, as compared to 30% without substance misuse. The group with combined problems also functioned most poorly.

People who combine dual diagnosis with a history of offending

The Revolving Doors Agency carried out a survey of arrests in Camden and Islington and identified 499 people (2% of all arrests) who had a mental health problem.[17] 61 members (12%) of the group had a record of offending, violence, drug or alcohol dependence, and losing contact with services. They often became homeless and had repeated contacts with the police.

People who need 24 hour nursed care

The group identified by the Department of Health as in need of 24 hour nursed care shares many characteristics with the client group for this Review. The Department of Health has defined the client group requiring 24 hour nursed accommodation as people with severe and long-term mental illness who need:

▷ daily monitoring of mental states;

▷ frequent monitoring of risk of either self-harm or violence towards others;

▷ storage, administration and supervision of medication which will usually be necessary on a daily basis;

▷ assistance with self-care and daily living skills;

▷ supervision and support to attend daycare or rehabilitation activities;

▷ crisis intervention at night if required;

▷ skilled management of challenging behaviour;

▷ possibly skilled management of dual or even triple diagnosis (i.e. combined drug and alcohol dependence and mental illness).[18]

The Department of Health estimates that about 13 per 100,000 of the adult population (10 per 100,000 of the general population) need such care, but also notes that there will be significant variations between districts. Again, the level of local social deprivation is a predictor of the rate of mental illness,[19] and in some metropolitan areas the prevalence of this group of clients may be four to five times the national average. Within some inner city districts, urban drift and social deprivation may increase the prevalence to 10 times the national average.

The Ritchie Report: the Special Supervision Group

The Ritchie Report on the care and treatment of Christopher Clunis identified a Special Supervision Group of 3,000 – 4,000 people nationally who require intensive care from a specialist team.[20] It was suggested that people should be included in this group if they shared at least two of the following factors:

▷ having been detained under the Mental Health Act (1983) more than once;

▷ a history of violence or persistent offending;

▷ having failed to respond to treatment from the general psychiatric services;

▷ being homeless.

This is the narrowest definition, and excludes many of the group with which this Review is concerned. It does, however, define the most demanding people who present the highest risks and cause the greatest concerns.

Top tier of the Care Programme Approach, Section 117 aftercare, and supervision registers

The Care Programme Approach (CPA) was introduced in 1992, and designed to include everyone in contact with specialist services. More recently, many services have introduced a tiered system, with the top tier applied to people with complex needs who require multi-agency input.

Section 117 aftercare applies to those people discharged from hospital on sections 3, 37, 47 and 48 of the 1983 Mental Health Act, and requires multi-disciplinary needs assessment and coordination of care. Its principles are very similar to the top tier of the CPA, but it applies to fewer people.

There is evidence that the top tier criteria are applied inconsistently. For example, in three localities within a single trust in London, with comparable deprivation, rates of the top tier are about 2.3, 6.9 and 10.2 per 1,000 of the adult population, with men and people from minority ethnic communities over-represented.[21]

Across several trusts in North London with comparable deprivation indices, between 20% and 50% of people on the top tier of the CPA were on section 117 aftercare. When a composite risk category was applied for people at risk of self-harm, self-neglect or harming others, this included between 0.25 and 0.5 per 1,000 of the adult population, a difference of a factor of 20, suggesting differences in application rather than genuine differences in need or risk.[22]

The supervision registers, introduced in 1994 for people who are being cared for in the community and have a severe mental illness, should be most pertinent to this Review. Three risk factors were identified:

▷ a significant risk of suicide;

▷ a significant risk of serious violence to others;

▷ a significant risk of severe self-neglect.

Nationally, there are about 4,000 people on supervision registers. However, the registers are used so inconsistently across the UK that they offer little indication of prevalence.[23]

The new long-stay psychiatric population

A recent study identified three main categories of new long-stay patients who cannot be discharged from hospital:

▷ patients who are so disabled by their psychiatric illness and concomitant physical illnesses that they require 24 hour nursing and medical care;

▷ patients who remain in hospital because their behaviour breaches the selection policies of community-based residential accommodation;

▷ patients for whom there is no alternative accommodation available in the community.[24]

For the purposes of this Review, the latter two subgroups are relevant. Recent work on the new long-stay psychiatric population found an average point prevalence of 8 per 100,000 of the adult population (6.1 per 100,000 of the general population).[25] A group requiring a high level of intensive support, but not necessarily hospital care, has been identified for many years. This group is severely disabled and is estimated to occupy 9% of hospital beds, or about 3,500 beds in England.[26]

Care management

An indication of social care need is the proportion of people with severe mental illness receiving care management from social services. This constitutes between 0.5-1% of the adult population across several trusts in North London. The variation is not explained by variations in need.[27]

Estimating the size of the client group for this Review

The group this Review is concerned with forms a mosaic of different needs and characteristics. One constant is that it includes people with severe and enduring mental illness who are difficult to engage, but who are clearly in need of care. In addition, they may be homeless, misusing substances, and perhaps have a history of offending and institutional care. Some may even be in hospital in the absence of proper community services. Section 117, the supervision registers, and the top tier of the CPA all include some of this group. Many are known to services, even if they are not in contact. Most are likely to be intermittently and chaotically in contact; others receive a confusing mixture of care which is not always effective or logical. Very few members of the group will be completely unknown to services.

All these groups are described by imprecise figures, varying nationally, and associated with the level of deprivation. Some estimates are possible, however. Prevalence of severe and enduring mental illness most likely varies between 0.3 -1.5% of the adult population. The group we are addressing is considerably smaller, probably about 5% of this group. This gives an average rate of **45 per 100,000 adult population** and a total figure for this group of approximately **15,000 people nationally.**

However, prevalence of this group will be strongly correlated to deprivation, since most predictive variables such as ethnicity, homelessness and drug misuse are associated with deprivation. Typically, **a deprived inner-city area might expect 200 people per 100,000 of the general population,** while a well-off suburban or rural area might only have a handful.

Conclusion

In this chapter we have introduced the client group as a set of people with multiple problems and complex long-term needs. We have suggested that the service response to this group is inadequate and that this is an issue which requires urgent and coordinated attention. We estimate that there may be about 15,000 people nationally in this group, often concentrated in deprived inner city areas. Chapter 2 goes on to look at some of the specific problems faced by the client group and some of the reasons why engagement is so often unsuccessful.

CHAPTER 2

The problems faced by the client group

This chapter aims to:

▷ **identify some of the problems faced by the client group;**

▷ **suggest why it is difficult for users to engage with services;**

▷ **analyse why it is also difficult for services to engage with users.**

2.1 The problems of the client group

The people in this client group suffer from a combination of detrimental and damaging characteristics which interact with each other. First, they suffer all the psychological, social and practical consequences of having a severe mental illness. They may also have additional difficulties such as substance misuse or homelessness, and in many cases they do not receive the care they need.

People in this group experience symptoms of mental illness which may be intense and frightening. They may hear constant threatening voices, or be convinced that others are trying to harm them. Sometimes this can lead to aggression. Many suffer from deep depressive feelings, and have suicidal ideas. Energy levels may be low. There may be an additional diagnosis of personality disorder, or people may suffer from the memories of a history of abuse and neglect. Many will not agree with professionals' views of the nature of their problems and will not accept that they need help.

A further complication concerns the social disabilities which may flow from mental health problems in the first instance, but can soon become serious difficulties in their own right. Nearly everybody in this group will be unemployed, and many will not take up all their benefits. Their housing will be marginal at best, but in many cases they will have unstable and inadequate accommodation or be homeless. People in this group are not able to be fully independent, and will frequently suffer neglect. This may lead to begging and petty crime. If they have children, they may have difficulties in looking after them and children may be taken into care. Many members of the group may have physical health problems which will often be ignored.

As if this were not enough, wider society reacts to this group (as to many people with mental health problems) in a way which may be excluding and rejecting. There is stigma surrounding mental illness which can make it doubly difficult to secure adequate housing, meaningful daytime activity, or even networks of friendship and support. In various studies it has been found that members of this group want what everybody else wants.[28] Most would like a decent home, a partner and a job, but their health problems, together with the factors described here, mean that their aspirations are not achieved.

The key to delivering the treatment and support this group requires is to understand the underlying incompatibility of what people in need want and what the services offer.

2.2 Why users find it difficult to engage with services

Suspicion of statutory services

Many of the people who fall within the remit of this Review may have had a range of unsatisfactory, and possibly traumatic, contacts with statutory services in the past. Some of these experiences may be directly connected with mental health services, such as:

▷ traumatic experiences of hospitalisation;

▷ bad experiences of the side-effects from medication;

▷ experience of being held under a section of the Mental Health Act 1983.

Other negative experiences of statutory services may range more widely:

▷ having been in local authority care as a child;

▷ having a child taken away by social services;

▷ experiences of racism and/or sexism from statutory services.

A significant proportion of the group will also have had negative experiences of the criminal justice system, perhaps including:

▷ experience of the youth justice system;

▷ bewildering experiences of arrest, court appearances, and remand to prison, perhaps during a mental health crisis.

Many members of this group will also have had:

▷ frustrating dealings with housing departments, perhaps leading to homelessness or inadequate accommodation;

▷ confusing experiences in trying to claim the benefits to which they are entitled.

A Sainsbury Centre report on users' experiences of living in the community identified particular problems in dealing with housing officials and the DSS. Lack of respect was mentioned frequently: "They treat you like a child or worse"; "They think they can put me at the back of the queue"; "I don't know my way around the bureaucracy and they just tell me to go away as if it's my fault that I don't understand".[29]

Users' views of services

To gain some sense of what service users themselves felt were the problems with services, the Review sought users' views in a small-scale exercise. Nine semi-structured interviews were carried out with a group of users who identified themselves as having some of the cluster of problems with which the Review was concerned. The interviews were carried out by user consultants.

The questionnaires were designed to create discussion around the following areas:

▷ what users' experience of the services offered to help them with their problems had been;

▷ which services had been the most helpful and useful and the reasons for this;

▷ which services had been the least helpful and useful and the reasons for this;

▷ the main barriers they had experienced in getting access to care.

Demographic information and the history of the person's illness were also obtained, although interviewees' names were kept confidential to the researchers.

A consistent theme throughout the interviews was the feeling that services were dehumanising and controlling. Black users, in particular, felt that their opinions were not listened to, and that they were not respected. There were also, however, frequent mentions of individual practitioners with whom users had had a good relationship and who had been genuinely helpful. User organisations were considered by one user to be the most helpful because "they value you for what you are".

Two users spoke of the difficulty they had in accessing services because they did not have a recognisable psychosis. One user said: "they can never seem to make up their minds whether or not I have a mental illness". She had been diagnosed as having a combination of depression and personality disorder: "[it's] probably that I am such a mixed bag, nobody knows where to start". She was critical of the statutory services because although there seemed to her to be effective treatment available, such as psychotherapy and hypnotherapy, they were not prepared to support her in these treatments. She had found statutory services generally unhelpful, but spoke highly of a voluntary service which could provide support to her at any time of the day or night.

Black users talked of the racism they had suffered both as citizens and as patients. One black user said that although he had been born in England, he had "never really felt part of this land. People see me as a problem before they see my problems". As patients they had been disempowered and made to feel helpless: "When I could not get the doctor to listen to me I asked my mother to ask the questions but she was made to feel foolish and helpless". One user spoke of the lack of West Indian food available in hospital.

Another user spoke of how his Rastafarian faith had helped him personally, although he felt that this was also a source of prejudice against him: "People don't like me because I am a black man who is a Rasta. If people would take some of my opinions I would improve. I am not a bad man, just a black man with some problems."

A number of users spoke of dreadful experiences of being in hospital. Black users spoke of being in locked hospital facilities as particularly bad experiences: "the Regional Secure Unit was the very worst".

Dislike of medication and being too heavily medicated were raised by several of the users: as one user put it, "I was changed into a shadow person who exists but does not live". Some users mentioned the lack of alternative treatments to medication and the lack of a holistic approach to treatment.

Whilst the group of users interviewed was small, their opinions are consistent with other user opinion surveys. What is of particular relevance to this Review is that what users appreciate is having staff who care, who listen and who understand their needs. It is the personal qualities and appropriate skills (such as understanding the needs of people from different cultural backgrounds) which are most important to users.

Fear of dying

Users' views of services were also discussed at the focus group on targeting services on black and minority ethnic communities. One of the most striking issues to emerge was that for many black users a key reason for non-engagement is quite literally a fear that involvement with mental health services will kill them. In evidence, examples of several deaths in hospital and prisons were given, some related to overprescribing of psychiatric medication, others to aggressive restraining techniques.

Racism, discrimination, and insensitivity to other cultures

Some of the negative experiences recorded above may have been due to racism, but they are also likely to flow from mental health workers' ignorance about, or insensitivity to, other cultures. This is a central issue for this client group, because of the evidence that people from black and minority ethnic communities are over-represented in the group.

Box 2. Mangal sutra

A 23 year old woman had a breakdown after divorce from her husband. She was admitted to hospital under section 3 of the Mental Health Act 1983 as she had repeatedly threatened to burn herself. Her family was in India and she did not know many people in England apart from her ex-husband's family. The young woman had been married for four years, and the grounds for the divorce were that she had been unable to conceive. She could not accept the divorce and often wandered the streets at night with a petrol can threatening to set herself alight.

In the hospital, the necklace she was wearing was taken away from her, in case she used it to strangle herself. The woman became extremely agitated and tried to throw herself out of a window. She was then sedated and kept under 24 hour supervision. She repeatedly asked for her necklace and her behaviour deteriorated. It was not until an Asian social worker visited her that it was understood that the necklace was a mangal sutra, worn only by married women. She had not stopped wearing it because she could not accept the divorce and the stigma attached to divorced women in the Hindu community.

There are several facets of the specific problems encountered by people from black and minority ethnic communities who do not engage with mental health services:

▷ racism is probably present in the mental health workforce and may have been even more prevalent when older users first came into contact with services;

▷ some mental health workers may feel that they hold different traditions in equal value to their own, but simply lack the knowledge to be sensitive in practice;

▷ mainstream services may be completely out of touch with black and minority ethnic communities.

In the future, it is essential that the mental health workforce has an adequate representation of people from these communities, but also that all workers receive training and awareness-raising in issues of cultural difference. **Boxes 2** and **3** contain two examples of cases where ignorance or insensitivity to cultural differences can have serious and sometimes tragic consequences.

Box 3. Interrogation

A 30 year old man from Somalia arrived in the UK and sought asylum. He had been imprisoned and tortured. He had been living on the streets for six months and had developed a chest infection. He was eventually helped by an outreach worker who booked him into a hotel. It was noted that the man had balance and communication difficulties. A social worker suggested that he see a community psychiatric nurse. He was also referred to the homeless unit.

He was diagnosed as having hearing loss, and, after referral to a specialist, arrangements were made to have an operation which would assist his hearing loss and balance difficulties. Whilst waiting for the operation, his health deteriorated. He was subjected to repeated questioning by the social worker, psychiatric nurse, and staff from the homeless unit. He started becoming very distressed about these visits and referring to them as "interrogations". He became verbally abusive and disturbed. He disappeared soon afterwards and was found dead three months later.

A recent Sainsbury Centre report has drawn attention to the major role of religion in many minority ethnic communities and the wide variety of faiths represented in these communities.[30] Understanding cultural differences is an essential part of community mental health services, but it is also important not to neglect the belief systems which underpin cultural identity and are an integral part of it.

Non-adherence to medication

Poor adherence to medication is a central factor in frequent breakdowns, poor functioning and danger to self and others.[31] It is estimated that as many as 80% of people with psychosis do not adhere to their treatment,[32] and this will be especially the case in this group. Side-effects are often given as reasons for discontinuation. It has also been argued that personal health beliefs and perceptions of illness will determine whether individuals undertake recommended treatment.[33,34] One study found that although the side-effects of treatment were important, other factors were also significant. These included:

▷ coming to terms with having a long-term illness which required long-term maintenance medication;

▷ establishing a trusting and continuous relationship with one or more care professionals;

▷ practical experience with various types of medication until one could be identified which had the fewest side-effects while maximising symptom control.[35]

What is needed is openness about what medication can achieve and what its effects are likely to be. Some of the key issues are set out below.

▷ Realistic expectations

Patients' expectations about medication are sometimes raised so that they look for rapid improvements in their wellbeing. Often these expectations are unrealistic. If people are promised improvements that do not materialise they feel let down or misled. This can start, or increase, a feeling of distrust of services. Where people are given a realistic impression of what drugs can and cannot achieve, how likely success is, and what alternatives are available if the treatment fails, agreement is more likely, and trust can be built.

▷ Side-effects

For many people, the most common reason for stopping medication is the range and severity of short-term side-effects. Many of these affect an individual's physical appearance, marking them out as different. This can increase their feelings of isolation, further damage their self-esteem, and open them to additional ridicule and abuse within the community. Patients are often given no indication in advance of the possible effects, how serious they may be, or what can be done to mitigate them. When the side-effects begin, people's first reaction is often to stop treatment at once.

It has been argued that switching non-adherent patients to atypical anti-psychotics will increase compliance because of their lower side-effect profile. Although this will be so in some instances, it is unlikely to be the answer to all problems in this area.

▷ **Long-term risks**

In addition to the immediate effects, people worry about the long-term risks associated with psychotropic drugs. If fears of damage to the heart, the liver, and the nervous system are ignored, then suspicion and dissent may follow. There is some evidence to suggest that newer anti-psychotics have fewer such consequences, but this is a research question that can only be answered with certainty over time.

▷ **Issues of power and control**

Medication in general, and depot injections in particular are, in the minds of many people who have been subject to aggressive treatment regimes, strongly linked to control and punishment. In these cases declining medication is as much about rejecting authoritarian control as denying therapeutic benefit.

2.3 Why services find it difficult to engage with users

The previous section looked at reasons for non-engagement from the point of view of service users. For the people working in mental health services, it is clear that this client group can be very difficult to work with and that the initial engagement may take many months of persistent effort. In addition, some structural issues are of key importance.

Difficulties of diagnosis and responsibility

The many problems and needs of this group require input from many agencies. Some of the responsibilities of these agencies are overlapping, and it is not always clear who should take responsibility as the lead agent. Since this group can be so challenging to engage, and hard to keep contact with, it can be tempting for agencies to deny their role, and try to shift the responsibility to another agency, as has been identified by many inquiries into mental health and social care. This is particularly detrimental to a group with such severe problems, and reluctance to receive care.

Distinguishing between mental health problems and social problems

Identification of problems and allocation of appropriate and effective care is essential. Clearly, mental health care should be targeted on those whose needs cannot be better met in any other way. For people whose problems are purely social, assessment by specialists in mental health can be stigmatising. Equally, it would be inappropriate for people with multiple social problems to be swept into the mental health system for no good reason other than the lack of alternative services to meet their needs.

The lack of such services, however, may be precisely the reason for some of the pressures and problems experienced by teams which are trying to provide a service to the client group for this Review. The Tulip Outreach Team and the Elmore Community Support Team are described elsewhere in this report (in **Chapter 4, Boxes 5** and **7**). These are examples of flexible independent sector services which can absorb some of the people who fall between the inclusion criteria of various statutory services. It seems likely that in any area where the client group for the Review is present in significant numbers, there will also be a number of people who fall between statutory services in this way unless their needs are specifically targeted. A strategic solution to this problem is to complement the specialist services with capacity and expertise aimed at the Review client group, whether in the statutory or independent sector.

Personality disorder

Personality disorder can be defined as "an enduring pattern of inner experience and behaviour that deviates markedly from the expectations of the individual's culture" (Diagnostic and Statistical Manual IV). It includes many different disorders ranging from histrionic personality to antisocial personality disorder (often referred to as psychopathic disorder). It is antisocial personality disorder that is most relevant to this Review. This topic has been discussed in depth by one of the working groups of the Reed Review.[36]

A diagnosis of personality disorder can lead to exclusion from care for a variety of reasons. Personality disorder can be specified as not being part of the remit of the service – that is, it is not considered a severe mental illness. It can be defined as untreatable, and therefore used as a reason for refusing care. Particular problems arise when a label of personality disorder is attached to a person because of difficult behaviour such as criminality, violence or substance misuse – all of which are associated with anti-social personality disorder – and as a consequence care is refused.

On the other hand, other agencies are often equally reluctant to engage with people with personality disorder because they consider them as mentally ill due to their long association with mental health care. This increases the risk that people fall between services. However, these are precisely the people who can create major difficulties for themselves, relatives and society, and unless the responsibility for, and details of, their care have been specified among the many organisations and individuals who can contribute, problems will escalate. Inquiries have repeatedly highlighted this problem.

These difficulties need to be addressed openly, and it has to be recognised that some service has to be responsible for this group. However, not all people and their difficulties, whether social or behavioural, can be accepted by mental health services. If people are to be excluded, the criteria and their reasons have to be made explicit in operational policies, and other available services should be identified to meet the needs of this group. If no such services exist, reasons should be given by the responsible commissioners.

Dual diagnosis of mental health and substance misuse problems

Debate continues about whether services for people with a dual diagnosis of mental illness and substance misuse should be integrated with mainstream services or provided by specialist teams. There are reports that problematic drug and alcohol use in combination with mental illness is increasing, so that it may not be a practicable solution in the future to provide separate services for this group of people. Increasing evidence is also available to suggest that an integrated service serves these people best since the problems of people in this group are similar in quality, but worse in intensity, compared to those who suffer the primary consequences of mental illness without substance misuse.[37,38]

Mainstream mental health services need to employ or have access to staff who have specialist skills in working with people who have both mental health and drug and alcohol problems. Accessibility of and acceptance by services are the keys to working with people who have dual problems, who are often among the most marginalised of service users.

People with dual diagnosis are likely to be particularly difficult to manage and hard to engage. Substance misuse is associated with exacerbation of symptoms, aggression and violence, with getting evicted, and with greater use of crisis services.[39] Substance misuse may threaten engagement in that people are less likely to adhere to medication or to keep appointments if they are frequently intoxicated and their lives and social groups are chaotic. Intoxication also makes it difficult for staff in day and residential services to manage members of this group. In services designed solely for people with substance misuse, staff generally tell people to go away if they are intoxicated, or eject them from residential services. It is much less clear what should be done with people who are also psychotic.

For services working with people with dual diagnosis, there are some major differences of approach that need to be reconciled. For instance, an element of coercion can be applied to mental health problems, whereas for drug and alcohol problems the philosophy is that clients take responsibility for themselves and treatment is exclusively voluntary.

A further conflict in approach occurs because mental health problems are perceived as illnesses and drugs may be prescribed as part of the treatment. However, if someone has a drug or alcohol problem, it is perceived as a behaviour over which they can take control and the use of any drugs is discouraged. In this context insisting on the taking of prescribed drugs can appear to be a conflict.

With clients who have both a mental health problem and a drug or alcohol problem these conflicting approaches to treatment can be difficult to resolve. One view is that a pragmatic approach to the use of alcohol and drugs by people with mental health problems needs to be developed, based on the philosophy of harm minimisation rather than expecting clients to abstain from use completely.

Organisation and aims of services

Members of the client group may sometimes fall between services in that they fail to meet the inclusion criteria for several different teams. Some of these issues could be addressed by the organisation of services along different lines – for example, by the provision of specialist teams targeted at the client group.

A number of other issues pertaining to the current organisation and aims of services seem of particular importance in analysing the difficulties of engagement.

▷ Services are focused on outcomes rather than engagement

Not surprisingly, given the systems of contracting and performance management within which they operate, services are driven to look at short-term outcomes in order to show that they are providing a valuable and effective service. For services which deal with the client group for the Review, however, this emphasis may often be unhelpful. The scope for short-term improvement may be limited. Success should perhaps be measured in terms of achieving initial engagement and gaining acceptance of what may seem fairly low-level interventions, and which may appear to have little to do with mental health. Giving primacy to engagement seems likely to address at least some of the reasons why people are avoiding services.

▷ Services may be too led by a model of mental illness

Linked to the need to focus on engagement is the need to start with help with practical matters. Although all members of the client group have a severe and long-term mental illness, the reasons why they resist engagement and have chaotic lives are wide-ranging. What is needed in the first instance may be help with housing, work, finances, benefits, childcare, and dealing with all the services and agencies that administer these areas. Stabilising these elements of a person's life may go a long way towards reducing the chaos whilst also opening a door for more traditional psychiatric interventions.

▷ Staff may not always be flexible enough in the way they work

If people working with the client group are to give primacy to engagement and practical help, they will need to be highly skilled and able to work in a flexible way. They need not necessarily be professional mental health workers, but if they are, they may have to be prepared to put some of their more specialist skills on hold in the early stages of the relationship with a client.

Clearly there are many people working in mental health services who are doing an excellent job. The discussions during the course of the Review were not conducted in a spirit of criticism of these workers. The key point is that the strategies of selection and training of the mental health workforce need to change in some areas so that the necessary range of skilled and sensitive staff is available.

Conclusion

The client group for the Review suffers from a plethora of problems and disadvantages. Although the reluctance of people in this group to engage with mental health services can be frustrating for staff, there are some valid reasons why they may feel suspicious of being drawn into this system of care. Services may also actively exclude people in the group because of the complexity and ambiguity of the clients' problems. The Review agreed that the needs of the group are not being met by current services in most areas, and that services are not being supported by the appropriate policy framework for this group. In Chapter 3 we sketch in the policy context and the current range of services available to the group, and analyse their adequacy.

CHAPTER 3

Current policy and services

This chapter:

▷ describes the policy context for the Review client group and assesses how successful it is;

▷ sketches in the service context and analyses how adequate current service provision is for this client group.

3.1 The policy context

There is little by way of national policy directed specifically towards the group for this Review. This is, perhaps, not surprising. Historically, policy – and services – have evolved gradually and policy development has often lagged behind scientific and social change. In the last ten years however, policy on mental health services has developed much more rapidly in response to growing professional and public concern about severe mental illness. Some of these developments are relevant to the current group, but no coherent service model has yet been promulgated.

Service development is perhaps slightly ahead of policy in that there are a number of initiatives which are particularly suitable for the group, including the establishment of assertive outreach teams and 24 hour nursed accommodation. These services have not been established on any consistent basis nationally.

The development of mental health policy

The development of mental health policies is a story, largely, of Ministers and officials rushing to catch up with social and service change. It was not until the 1960s that it became official policy to run down the old long-stay institutions, although this process had been underway for a decade and the evidence and rationale for closure was already clear. In the 1970s and early 1980s there was a gradual development of community care policies for mentally ill people, centred initially on acute District General Hospital psychiatric units and community mental health teams – although the latter were slow to develop. At this stage there was very limited thought about how the most disabled individuals would be accommodated within the system. In any case, enough long-stay beds remained to absorb this pressure.

It was not until the late 1980s that it became widely recognised that there is a cohort of highly disabled severely mentally ill people with multiple needs, who require specialised and intensive support, and that there are new recruits to this cohort who have not been residents of the old long-stay hospitals. It was also increasingly recognised that institutionalisation, although relevant, was not the cause of multiple disabilities in the group. This was predictable, but until it became evident that people in this group were living in the community and that their needs were not being systematically met, there was no pressure to address the problem or even to understand its origins. The group for this Review forms a key subset of this wider group to which policy and services have had to respond over the last ten years. **Appendix 5** contains a chronological summary of policy developments in recent years.

Current policy for the Review client group

It is perhaps unfair to attempt to construct an implied policy model for the group considered by the Review from the variety of policy initiatives in recent years, as these have had to address far wider issues. However, although there is no precise and evidence-based service model for the group, there are some general principles which can be deduced. The four key principles in policy seem to be:

▷ **A suitable range of services needs to be in place**

This has been summarised most recently in the 1996 document *The Spectrum of Care*.[40] This emphasises the need for 24 hour nursed care, crisis services and intensive home support as part of a full range of mental health services. The need for 24 hour nursed care was specifically emphasised at around the same time by a separate publication on this subject.[41] This included an action plan for the NHS Executive and local agencies. *The Spectrum of Care* also emphasises the need for day services and employment opportunities. Recent statements by Ministers have also stressed the importance of 24 hour nursed care, although no systematic plans for building up the level of this element of the care spectrum have yet been advanced.

▷ **Care planning must be carried out on a consistent basis and services must be coordinated across a range of agencies**

Policy on care planning started to be promulgated in 1991 with the Care Programme Approach (CPA) and has evolved continuously since then.[42] The CPA emphasises the need to:

▷ assess health and social care needs systematically;

▷ formulate a care plan;

▷ appoint a key worker – usually a mental health nurse or social worker;

▷ review the care plan regularly.

Unfortunately, introduction of the CPA was:

▷ not coordinated with the introduction of care management under the NHS and Community Care Act 1990;

▷ not prioritised for the most needy clients when first introduced, but was intended to apply to all patients in contact with specialist services.

Building Bridges attempted to address this in 1995 by suggesting the use of a tiered CPA (with only the most needy clients receiving a full multi-disciplinary CPA), and encouraging the coordination of care management and the CPA.[43] It also emphasised the need for mental health workers to have high quality professional supervision and clear lines of accountability.

At a strategic level there has also been a recent emphasis on the joint commissioning of services for severely mentally ill people across health and social services.[44]

▷ **The most needy or severely disabled clients should be prioritised**

It was clear fairly early on that if the most disabled clients, including the group for this Review, were to receive adequate care, prioritisation would be required. This concept was introduced in 1991 in *The Health of the Nation* White Paper,[45] and developed subsequently through a number of mechanisms including supervision registers.[46] The Audit Commission report *Finding a Place* found weak targeting of severely mentally ill people by community mental health teams, but there was little analysis of whether this was due to inadequate management, or whether the service model was wrong and greater provision of assertive outreach and crisis services was required.[47] The latter was, however, supported as a way of reducing reliance on expensive hospital stays of dubious effectiveness.

▷ **Risk must be assessed and managed**

This is at the heart of the discharge guidance (1993)[48] and the introduction of supervision registers (1994).[49] The former describes how to assess risk, and the latter are intended primarily to prioritise care for those who are at risk, although there is evidence that they are not being used in a consistent way across the country.[50] There have also been central training initiatives in this area.[51]

In addition, there has been a limited amendment to the 1983 Mental Health Act in the form of supervised discharge.[52] The Mental Health Act does not (and probably cannot) provide for the prospective detention of individuals who do not currently require detention on the grounds of health or safety but may do so in the future. Neither does it provide for compulsory treatment in the community. There has been concern from some quarters that some severely mentally ill people, particularly in the client group for this Review, may not comply with medication and so may require either (or both):

▷ compulsory treatment in the community;

▷ rapid admission to hospital when it appears that they will break down.

In response to this perception, the previous administration introduced supervised discharge. This is essentially a form of guardianship to be operated by healthcare staff and allows a degree of legal control over residence, daycare and attendance for treatment. It does not, however, allow compulsory treatment or prospective hospital admission. The rationale seems to be that it will encourage compliance with treatment, and some clinicians have found it helpful for this purpose, but it has not been widely used. It is unclear what the benefits are if a patient is placed on supervised discharge but still fails to comply with the treatment regime. It would appear that the new Government may be planning to embark on a review of the Mental Health Act 1983, but the form this will take is not yet known.

Current policy has not met the needs of the Review client group

It is easy to criticise policy, but much harder in practice to construct policies which work coherently across organisational boundaries for every client group. The group under consideration here poses particular challenges.

All the policies described above arguably have some merit as far as the group is concerned. The emphasis on consistent care planning and targeting has been particularly important in informing local service development and the move to the tiered CPA has been widely welcomed. The main elements of the CPA are clearly relevant to the group, as are many of the principles of care management, communication and coordination set out in *Building Bridges*. Similarly, the need for a range of services and for adequate risk assessment is clear. However, there are gaps and confusions in policy and the way in which it can address the needs of the group.

▷ No clear service model

One specific problem is that the service model is unclear. People working in the field have been confused by being told on the one hand that they must target community mental health teams on the most needy individuals, and on the other that they must develop specialist crisis services and 24 hour nursed care. The evidence-base for using the latter model for the whole of the client group is unclear, and the economics and practicalities have not been addressed. Attempting to provide 24 hour nursed care for the whole client group would represent an expensive, capital-led, strategy which does not appear to address the nature, needs and aspirations of much of the client group. This does not detract from the importance of such provision as part of the basket of required services.

▷ No consistent strategy for managing risk

Related to this, there is no consistent overall strategy for managing risk. Supervision registers are a bureaucratic mechanism – and one which is being used inconsistently across the country – to identify individuals who are at risk, but there is less in policy about how and with what tools to manage risk. Risk management cannot take place in a vacuum, but requires adequate services and skilled staff.

▷ No timetable for service development

Finally, and crucially, there is no feasible plan to put the required systems in place within a sensible timescale. Without such a plan there can never be a guarantee that individuals' needs can be met. For example, there is little point in pressing for more 24 hour nursed beds if no financial or human resources are available to make them a reality.

There are few examples within mental health of Government becoming involved directly in helping to develop services – the Mental Illness Specific Grant is one instance. Often it is right for Government to set only the broad agenda because detailed service planning is best done locally. In this case, however, the urgency, the small and complex nature of the group, and the requirement for cross-agency coordination, suggest that a stronger lead is required from the centre.

The questions which policy needs to address

Future policy development must pay more attention to developing the mechanisms for meeting the needs of the group, and to assembling these within each authority. Basic requirements of policy include:

▷ **stating a clear service model towards which services should work.** This report puts forward such a model. Whether this is accepted in whole or part, greater clarity is needed from the centre about what is required locally;

▷ **identifying the service features which will successfully meet needs.** These will include features such as a capacity for long-term engagement and out-of-hours cover, and attention to social factors as well as the medical factors. They will include features already usefully identified in the CPA and subsequent guidance;

▷ **putting in place a national strategy for delivering these services.** This requires attention to the financial, human resources, legal and administrative framework. It will need effective joint working across Government Departments and strong performance management by Regional Offices. It is no easy task, but the aim of this report is to help the process by starting to set the agenda.

The impact of recent generic policy developments

The White Paper on the NHS sets out a long-term agenda for the structural development of the NHS.[53] This is helpful inasmuch as it provides a clear context for service development for this client group. It will be important to ensure that the needs of the group do not get lost in the rush to develop locality commissioning. This should be possible given the preference for retaining mental health Trusts and the strategic lead for Health Authorities. It will be vital for Health Authorities to take the lead in commissioning services for this group if momentum is to be maintained.

The Green Paper on public health may also provide a useful framework for addressing the mental and physical health promotion needs of severely mentally ill people at a strategic level. The presence of such a framework should be one of the criteria for evaluating this document.

3.2 The service context

Our finding that there is little national policy directed specifically at the client group was reflected in our review of the services currently available. In most areas, members of this challenging and needy group are supposed to have their needs met through generic community mental health services, inpatient care, and whatever range of residential care is available.

For the Review, the key questions about the range of services available to the group are:

▷ can they achieve engagement?

▷ do they offer sufficient intensity of contact and levels of support?

▷ do they enable clients to access the range of other necessary services such as support with daily living, daytime activity, and help with accommodation, finance and benefits?

Community Mental Health Teams

In most areas, Community Mental Health Teams (CMHTs) are the central component of services for people with mental health problems living in the community.[54] CMHTs can offer a good standard of service to many people with severe mental illness, but cannot provide the central plank of services for the client group for the Review because:

▷ members of CMHTs have caseloads that are too high to allow intensive contact;

▷ the style of service delivery may not be assertive enough;

▷ the skill-mix of CMHTs may not be the most suitable for the client group.

Some areas have developed **specialist teams** for working with severely mentally ill people: these include:

▷ case management teams for severely mentally ill people;

▷ rehabilitation teams;

▷ assertive outreach teams;

▷ home care teams.

Specialist teams are more likely to be able to offer the intensive and assertive contact needed by the group. However, although there are no national data available on the numbers of specialist community teams, including assertive outreach teams, it is clear that only a minority of districts have these. In areas where community teams have not developed, a more **hospital-based rehabilitation service** remains.

Crisis services

Members of the client group require some form of 24 hour cover. Across the country, arrangements for the management of crisis vary. In some areas the provision is very limited. In a Sainsbury Centre study 60% of a sample of districts relied solely on a system of on-call medical staff who could be accessed through the A&E Department at the local hospital.[55] The remaining 40% had developed a mixture of cover through specialist teams, extended cover from CMHTs, helplines and crisis services.

Access to primary health care

Many members of the client group have poor access to primary healthcare for a variety of reasons including reduced mobility, lack of social skills, and being denied access. People with long-term mental illness are particularly vulnerable to physical health problems and it is estimated that up to 45% are likely to have severe concurrent physical morbidity.[56] The mortality rate of patients with schizophrenia is twice the normal rate, due in part to respiratory and cardiovascular disease. It is therefore essential that members of the client group are registered with a GP and have access to primary care to address their physical health care needs.

Daytime activity

Daytime activity has a major role in care of the client group, but while there has been some growth in daycare and work provision, users still complain of a shortage of satisfying daytime activities. Work schemes and day services seem to suffer some problems in motivating many of their users, and some may exclude the client group for this Review.

Welfare advice

Help with finance and benefits is a high priority with service users generally, and is particularly important for this client group, many of whom have serious problems in this area. The stigmatising language used in official leaflets can be a disincentive to people taking up benefits. A national survey following the introduction of Disability Living Allowance and Disability Working Allowance found that people with certain specific types of disability were more likely to attract a lower rate or no benefit at all.[57] This included people with mental health problems, particularly agoraphobia and schizophrenia. A lack of understanding by the adviser of the effects of the disability was sometimes a greater problem than the way the claimants completed the forms.

There is evidence that receipt of benefits by people with mental health problems is much less than entitlement. For example, one study of people attending a mental health resource centre found that 51% of attenders were not receiving the benefits to which they were entitled.[58] Whether or not people had a care manager did not affect their entitlement and it was considered that even if social workers had the knowledge to help with benefits claims, they did not have the time to provide the necessary input. The absence of widely accessible services to help people with severe mental illness receive their welfare entitlement is another problem for the Review client group.

Accommodation options

In the past, most people with severe and enduring mental health problems were looked after in the old long-stay hospitals. Mental health services have had to strike a difficult balance in developing community services while also sustaining a sufficient **range of residential care options** for those who cannot manage without on-site support. The number of hospital beds has been reduced although residential care places have increased, with new places provided by local authorities and the independent sector.[59] Partly as a result of this shift of provision away from the NHS, many residential care facilities do not have the staffing levels to provide 24 hour cover or adequate support to members of the Review client group.

For many people with severe mental illness, ordinary housing may be the best accommodation option, provided that appropriate levels of support are made available. For the Review client group, however, there are some special requirements. The support needs to be:

▷ intensive;

▷ continuing;

▷ available 24 hours per day;

▷ provided by adequately trained and supervised staff.

Three main options for the Review group have been identified:

▷ supported housing;

▷ 24 hour nursed care;

▷ ordinary housing with intensive support.

Supported housing has integrated care services, provided either by the landlord or under contract by a separate agency. The service may range from initial resettlement support to 24 hour cover involving intensive care services. The type of housing provided can range from ordinary self-contained housing to specialist accommodation, such as a hostel or residential care home. Most supported housing provided by housing associations is managed by specialist independent organisations.

Supported housing tends to be attractive to service users, who often prefer independent living in accommodation where staff visit. Flexible support can be provided which is tailored to individual needs. On the other hand, some disadvantages of this option have been identified:

▷ many housing workers have not received training in mental health issues;[60]

▷ adequate support for clients living independently needs coordination; some services do not have the necessary mechanisms to achieve this;

▷ many supported housing projects rely on housing benefit to fund support and counselling, but the Department of Social Security is reviewing this practice; this area of uncertainty has already affected the viability of some projects;[61]

▷ this particular client group is likely to require a high level of support, which some schemes do not offer.

24 hour nursed care (also known as hospital hostels) has been recommended by the Department of Health as an essential service component for meeting the needs of people with severe mental illness and high support needs. Although the need to expand this type of provision has been stressed repeatedly by the Department, it remains scarce.

The Review was impressed by a scheme in Nottingham which offers **intensive support at home** to clients who would otherwise be in residential care. A description of this service is given in **Box 10** in **Chapter 5.** In brief terms, the support is given by teams of workers with very small protected caseloads. Clients can have a large number of contacts per week if necessary. This type of scheme does not seem to be common.

For some members of the client group with **accommodation problems** the need for suitable accommodation is desperate. They may be inappropriately housed in bed and breakfast accommodation, using direct access hostels, or sleeping rough. A number of cities have responded to the needs of homeless mentally ill people. In London, the Homeless Mentally Ill Initiative was set up in 1990 in response to widespread concern about the increase in the numbers of homeless and mentally ill people on the streets of central London.[62] Members of the client group who become street homeless are likely to require assertive and persistent outreach if they are to be engaged with mental health services.

An essential component of any service is the provision of **hospital beds** and secure accommodation. The reduction in hospital beds is well-known and there are now only 37,000 beds available. In the absence of fully developed community services, pressure on beds has increased constantly and occupancy rates of well over 100% have been reported. The direct relationship between the availability of community services and the pressure on hospital beds is clear.

Secure accommodation is a necessary component of services for a very small proportion of the Review client group. In response to recent policy and funding initiatives, the number of beds available in medium secure units has risen to 1,200.[63] Medium secure units are not intended to provide long-term care, however, and there are gaps in provision for people who require medium secure care in the longer term.

Services for offenders with mental health problems

Given that many members of the client group have a history of offending, the interface with wider services for offenders with mental health problems is of particular importance. Secure provision is one part of this network, and court diversion schemes play a central role. In a recent study, 59% of services reported having a scheme to identify and divert people with a mental health problem from the courts or police custody into specialist mental health services.[64] Unless there are appropriate and intensive community services available, members of the client group who are identified by such schemes may often slip out of contact with services rapidly.

Services for people with dual diagnosis

The interface of mental health services with substance misuse services is also of key importance to the client group. Services for people with a dual diagnosis of mental illness and substance misuse tend not to be integrated. Attempts at integration may meet some deep philosophical barriers in the approaches adopted in two separate services.

Overview

The consensus view of the Review team was that in many areas current services are not able to meet the needs of this client group. This is not necessarily the fault of individual staff, providers or commissioners. On the contrary, many are trying hard to address these complex needs. However, the design, quantity, style and nature of current services seem to fall short of what is required.

Conclusion

The Review looked at current policy and services and concluded that policy needs to be strengthened for this client group, and that there are notable service gaps. We used our analysis of the client group's needs and our survey of current provision to establish a service model of what should be in place for this group. We turn to this model in the next two chapters. Chapter 4 focuses on assertive outreach. Chapter 5 addresses key points in the range of other essential services such as accommodation, daytime activity and welfare advice.

CHAPTER 4

Essential services: assertive outreach

This chapter:

▷ describes assertive outreach and discusses the evidence for its effectiveness;

▷ gives guidance on developing an assertive outreach service;

▷ outlines the work, composition and training of assertive outreach teams, including the role of outreach workers.

Chapter 4 should be read in conjunction with Chapter 5, which goes on to discuss the equal importance of services to provide accommodation, daytime activity, and welfare advice.

Box 4. What the client group needs from services

- ► Engagement
- ► A range of treatments and care, including crisis intervention
- ► An identified person responsible 24 hours per day
- ► A risk management approach that offers safety for the client and the public
- ► Attention to social factors as well as the mental and medical problems
- ► Supported access to mainstream services
- ► Daytime activity giving occupation, opportunity and purpose
- ► Help with finance and benefits
- ► Suitable accommodation

4.1 The service model

Based on the previous chapters, a model of care emerges that offers sensitive but intensive care. Special attention needs to be given to the engagement of service users from a range of ethnic and cultural backgrounds. Although engagement should be perceived as a successful outcome in its own right, it is also a means towards the end of providing high quality and comprehensive care.

We have identified the main needs of the client group in **Box 4.** The challenge for any system of care is to meet these needs in such a way that all components are offered by people who have expertise in these areas, while avoiding fragmentation of service provision.

Clearly these needs could be met in a variety of ways. The service model that most impressed us by its suitability for the client group, however, is **assertive outreach** (or intensive case management). We explore this service function in some detail in this chapter. We were also convinced that assertive outreach must not be seen in isolation from the wider spectrum of services needed by the group. These services are summarised in **Table 1.**

Planning principles

The principles which should underpin the planning of services for this group should be based on:

▷ information through a local **needs assessment** of the numbers and needs of local people falling within the definition of the client group;

▷ **benchmarking of existing resources** which meet, or fail to meet, the needs of this group;

▷ urgent implementation of a modern **IT system** which supports a recurring cycle of needs assessment, audit, review and development to ensure services are most appropriately developed in each local situation;

▷ the establishment of an inter-agency, multi-disciplinary **assertive outreach** system with agreed local objectives and targets;

▷ **clearly designated local responsibilities** invested in a local individual or group of appropriate stakeholders.

Table 1. Services required to support the client group for the Review

Community support:	Primary care Crisis intervention Community-based alternatives to acute care Assertive outreach Support with daily living Generic community mental health services
24 hour care, residential provision, and housing:	Ordinary housing with intensive support Sheltered accommodation Group homes / shared housing Low support hostels Medium support hostels Residential homes High support accommodation 24 hour nursed accommodation Acute inpatient care Low secure units Medium secure units Special Hospitals
Daycare and daytime activities:	Ordinary employment Supported employment Adult education Employment rehabilitation places Clubhouse Day centre Day hospital Drop-in centre
Financial support:	Welfare advice service

The essential services for the client group

As stated above, we believe that assertive outreach is the core function required for the group, and in this chapter we offer evidence for this approach and practical guidance about implementation. We were equally strongly convinced that assertive outreach will not be effective in isolation from the other essential services summarised in **Table 1.** These are discussed in Chapter 5 and include the accommodation options for the group, the provision of welfare advice, and access to good daycare and employment schemes.

We are also convinced that service delivery can only be as good as the quality of its practitioners. Assertive outreach, and in fact any other form of mental health care, cannot simply be expected to be undertaken well because a group of highly motivated and committed people has been recruited. Staff should expect appropriate training and support if they are to be effective. We continue to be amazed about the expectations regarding the practice of assertive outreach and locally based mental health care, without the preparation and investment this requires in attitudinal change, skills and services. Staff requirements and their training needs are also presented in this chapter.

In this chapter and in Chapter 5 we draw on research evidence and on examples of creative service responses. Not all service examples have been evaluated by the Review, and we do not offer an exhaustive survey of the evidence on effectiveness.

4.2 The assertive outreach model

Several terms are used to describe assertive outreach, including intensive case management. For the purposes of this Review we consider them as identical.

We have found strong evidence which demonstrates the effectiveness of intensive community support for people with severe mental illness who have difficulty in accessing or accepting services. This is especially the case for services applying assertive outreach approaches where staff have low caseloads.[65,66,67,68] The evidence of good outcomes from assertive outreach models is clear in at least one respect: such specialist teams can engage and maintain contact with many of even the most difficult service users.[69] Typically, studies have shown that at least 95% of clients are still in contact with services even after 18 months.

Client characteristics and needs

Many assertive outreach teams deliberately select people who have the most severe and complex problems.[70,71,72] The typical user of these services can be described as "a single male in his early thirties who had been suffering from a schizophrenic illness for over a decade". More than 80% of service users have at least one of the following factors: "history of self-harm, history of violence, non-compliance with medication, non-cooperation with mental health services or admission within the past two years".[73]

The needs of these people are very severe. In an inner city study, assistance with housing difficulties was needed for 40% of clients, almost two-thirds needed help with benefits, and just under half required help with finances.[74] One in six needed support from forensic services, and one in three needed assistance with problems such as personal hygiene, shopping and cooking. Several patients required daily visits for several weeks during which time the necessary skills could be taught and reinforced. It was important not to exclude clients' families: almost two-thirds of relatives required support.[75]

Working practices

Central to the model of assertive outreach is the relationship between the staff member and client, described by service users as the "cornerstone of the care".[76] This requires high staff-user ratios, typically a maximum caseload of 15 clients, and sometimes 10 clients or even fewer. Staff provide considerable face-to-face care when necessary, and the approach is broad and client-centred. Specific interventions or treatments are a key component of the model, but the emphasis is placed on care coordination and advocacy.

Usually no formal purchasing is undertaken, although this is possible if social workers or other team members are care managers and have access to social services budgets. Equally important is liaison and cooperation between the team and GPs, who play an important role in providing general healthcare for the client group. Registration with a GP can be a problem, since many of the clients do not have a permanent home.

Working hours of most services are flexible, although 24-hour services are rare. It is essential that some form of back-up from easily accessible and well-informed staff is available.[77,78]

This approach requires a multi-disciplinary team including psychiatrists, mental health nurses and social workers. Some team members have no formal professional qualifications. These staff are of particular importance in the engagement process, and this will be discussed later in the chapter. The team leader plays an important role in inspiring and supervising the team, and maintaining fidelity to the purpose of the programme.

Teams function best if all staff are responsible managerially to the team leader, rather than having to report to a range of professional supervisors. This does not of course exclude accountability for actions to professional bodies.

Academics in the US have argued that any deviation from a pure model of assertive community treatment prevents achievement of the desired outcome.[79,80] A checklist of the key elements of assertive outreach forms **Appendix 6** of this report.

Effectiveness and cost

Evidence from assertive outreach allowed us to reach the conclusion that these services are effective for service users beyond their success with engagement. There is evidence from the US, Australia and the UK that symptomatology and social functioning of users improves, although gains are generally limited.[81,82,83] Clients receiving assertive outreach report high satisfaction with services and improved quality of their lives.[84] The Tulip Outreach Team in London is an example of a well-targeted and effective service. Brief details are given in **Box 5.**

Box 5. The Tulip Outreach Team

A recent Sainsbury Centre report looked at several teams providing support to people with mental health problems in the inner London Borough of Haringey.[85] The Tulip Outreach Team is an independent, non-profit-making organisation funded by health and social services, which provides intensive community support to people who are falling between the gaps of conventional services. The team is targeted at people with severe and enduring mental health problems, who are mostly of minority ethnic origin, and are homeless, or in danger of becoming so.

Tulip has small caseloads of about 10 clients per worker, and uses assertive outreach. The team operates a no-close policy so that clients who lose contact do not need to be re-referred. Clients can also be reassured that long-term support is available. One distinctive feature of the team is the use of the "team approach", which means that all team members work with all clients and workers do not carry individual responsibility.

The Sainsbury Centre study found that the Tulip Team was successful in engaging most of the clients who were appropriately referred (94%). Homelessness was reduced from 60% at referral to 33% at 12 months. The Team was also able to achieve accurate targeting of its service at people from ethnic minority communities who were in danger of becoming homeless.

The benefits of assertive outreach approaches can be greater for some users than others. Young people with higher levels of symptoms showed the greatest improvement in some services.[86] Another study offers anecdotal evidence that "former revolving door patients who had been reluctant to engage with services and whose illnesses were responsive to standard treatments did well, [but that] the service had little to offer patients with severe and intractable illness".[87]

We found strong evidence that assertive outreach teams reduce bed use. Research studies, with their special commitment to reduce bed use and their relatively brief lifespan, have achieved reductions of as much as 80%.[88,89,90] Regular services, such as the service in North Birmingham, are still able to achieve considerable reduction in bed use for their clients – about 50% (see **Box 6** later in this chapter).

Equally consistent in research reports is the finding that assertive outreach is more efficient than hospital-based care and costs less per person. Savings can vary depending on the intensity and quality of care, and savings ranging from 40% to 1-2% have been reported.[91,92,93,94] We are aware that such findings about savings cannot simply be generalised to the NHS. However, reports from sites such as North Birmingham suggest to us that the introduction of assertive outreach can produce some bed savings, and can pay for itself. We are also aware that the introduction of these services requires an initial investment, for example in the form of bridging funding.

Assertive outreach teams improve access to housing, occupation and financial support.[95,96,97] However, little progress can be anticipated if staff lack the necessary expertise, or if the resources in the community (housing, for example) are insufficient or inadequate.[98] Locally based care in general, and assertive outreach in particular, will only be as good as the staff providing it and the community supporting it. These key issues are addressed later in the report.

It may be helpful to observe the factors that are associated with locally based care that does not produce good outcomes. Where assertive outreach has been ineffective, several consistent factors have emerged including:

▷ the assertive outreach team adopts a brokerage model of care and is not the main provider of services, including clinical interventions;[99,100]

▷ teams are not multi-disciplinary and receive inadequate training and supervision;[101,102]

▷ the team does not have control over hospital admissions;[103]

▷ assertive treatment is not combined with other relapse prevention techniques.[104]

Continuity of care

An essential aspect of effective assertive outreach is continuity of care, including continuity across community and hospital. If reductions in bed use are to be achieved, hospital stays need to be prevented or shortened. This should not, of course, be to the detriment of service users or their carers. Therefore, teams need to be able to take responsibility for admission and discharge planning, and to be closely involved with the care users receive during an inpatient stay.

The best way to achieve this in practice is for a psychiatrist to be an active member of the team. The psychiatrist should have continuity of responsibility for care wherever care is taking place, both in hospital and the community. Many specific responsibilities can be passed on to other team members, and in some teams other staff can decide about the need to admit or discharge. If continuity of responsibility is not in place, admissions remain long, with loss of integration of care and lack of clarity about the boundaries of responsibility.[105]

The effects of assertive outreach tend to dissipate quickly after the intervention stops.[106] Sustained long-term care is therefore what is required, even though the intensity of care and style and type of intervention should regularly be reviewed according to the needs of the clients.

User views on assertive outreach

We are unaware of assertive outreach services that are not appreciated by their clients, and they are generally preferred to standard psychiatric care. Service users value most of all the relationship with staff. In a Sainsbury Centre study, many said that they considered team members to be their friends. They greatly valued the opportunities provided for change, and the reliability of team contacts.[107]

A second theme in studies of user views is that case managers can empower users, listen to their views and allow them to progress at their own pace. The Sainsbury Centre study noted that,

> By allowing people gradually to build up to taking their own decisions – by letting people take back control over their actions – staff were helping people back into the world and relieving not only their sense of isolation but their sense of shame.

A further important theme, and one that is a constantly mentioned by users, is the need for practical help, such as help with housing and finance. Staff advocate for their clients with DSS and housing providers as well as providing practical help such as mending a front door. To quote the study of users' views mentioned above,

> The relief of knowing that there was someone available to sort out these practical issues was a major factor in helping people to keep well and out of hospital. Knowing that staff were reliable, readily available, willing to tackle a problem about a bill or a difficult negotiation about medication, and provide a therapeutic listening ear, gave people the confidence to tackle the challenges of living in the community.

Helping service users to gain confidence to take part in mainstream activities in the community is an important feature of a team's work. Staff meet clients in pubs and cafés or facilitate small groups of users to meet each other in ordinary venues. They enable clients to take part in leisure activities such as swimming and bowling. Sometimes a budget is available to pay for items such as course fees for further education.

Relatives' satisfaction with this type of service is another theme that emerges constantly. Relatives invariably prefer assertive outreach and the support it offers them to their experience of family members having frequent hospital admissions.

Conclusions about the evidence on assertive outreach

Several conclusions can be drawn:

▷ assertive outreach teams can achieve engagement for 95% of people with the greatest difficulties;

▷ these services are effective and efficient and liked by users and carers;

▷ low caseloads are an essential feature of assertive outreach;

▷ assertive outreach is only as good as the services that are available locally;

▷ a full range of social, rehabilitative and treatment services is required;

▷ continuity and integration of care are essential components, both over time and across all services, including hospital and the community;

▷ as far as possible these services should be provided directly by the team, rather than the team merely brokering care, so as to avoid creating multiple interfaces;

▷ a multi-disciplinary group of staff should carry out the assertive outreach function, covering the essential skills.

4.3 Developing an assertive outreach function

Striking a balance with local needs and service configurations

Nationally, there are large variations in service configurations for the Review client group and for wider mental health services. It is vital that local need, social context, geography, resources and existing service structures are taken into account in developing suitable assertive outreach systems.

An important decision related to local need is the balance between integration and sensitivity. The more integrated the service is into the mainstream mental health services, the fewer the boundaries, and the easier the relationships. The downside is that the service will function as part of the mainstream and will be seen in this way by the service users – who are already reluctant to engage with mainstream services. A service might need to be set up at arms length, so that it is perceived as offering a different attitude and enhanced opportunities. Such a service can also generate creative tension with mainstream services, while allowing for the possibility of convergence and integration over time.

Different approaches for areas of greater and lesser need

We believe that in some areas, particularly those with higher numbers of the Review client group, only the establishment of a dedicated assertive outreach system will meet the needs of the area appropriately. In others, with a lower prevalence, the most appropriate action may be a re-examination of resource deployment and the introduction of realistic and pragmatic initiatives which build on existing local configurations.

Table 2 suggests different approaches which might be adopted in areas of high, moderate and low morbidity.

A dedicated assertive treatment team would be distinct from:

▷ a **crisis team** responsible for people at times of breakdown for a limited period;

▷ a **community mental health team** (CMHT) offering interventions to relatively stable people referred by primary care, with staff caring for as many as 60 patients each;

▷ a **continuing care team** responsible for stable patients who are highly dependent.

Table 2. Different approaches to developing the assertive outreach function in relation to local need

High morbidity	Moderate morbidity	Low morbidity
1 Development of an assertive outreach system to include multi-disciplinary assertive treatment.	1 Specially trained assertive outreach workers in appropriate numbers within a generic CMHT.	1 Agreed caseload / case-mix of severely mentally ill clients for generic CMHT plus accessible routes into the rehabilitation service.
2 Health and social services integrated within team.	2 Close joint working with crisis, rehabilitation and forensic community outreach teams.	2 Some reconfiguration and retraining of rehabilitation services.
3 Formally agreed sessional input from local special housing needs workers, welfare benefits workers, adult education, local daycare and occupational providers.	3 Sessional input from welfare benefits workers, housing workers, etc. or liaison / link worker system with locality neighbourhood offices, adult education, local voluntary and statutory sector services.	3 Sessional input from welfare benefit workers etc.,
4 Sessional input from a GP to provide physical care.		4 Liaison / link worker system with other agencies.

All these other functions are also an important part of the system.

Assertive outreach teams have a continuing responsibility for a semi-permanent group of people. This group is identified in part by the challenge it poses to services. If stabilised, people can be referred either to the CMHT or to the continuing care team, and, in exceptional cases, to primary care. However, it is likely that most will remain users of the outreach team for many years. The service in North Birmingham described in **Box 6** is an example of such a service model.

In contrast, a rural area might incorporate assertive outreach as one of the functions of the regular CMHT, since the population is too thinly spread out and the prevalence of such challenging people too low to support a variety of specialist teams.

In areas of moderate deprivation and prevalence, reconfiguration or reorganisation is possible in a variety of ways. Crisis services can be combined with assertive outreach, or the function can be coordinated between a crisis service and a continuing care team. Sometimes a small, specialised outreach team can be commissioned from the independent sector, with explicit criteria about inclusion, exclusion and mutual responsibilities with, and accountability to, the statutory sector. It is not the structure that determines the effectiveness, but how the tasks are being delivered, provided care is in accordance with the principles described earlier in the chapter.

The Assertive Outreach Team was developed as part of a staged approach to service reconfiguration. First, the Psychiatric Emergency Team (PET) was established. This multi-disciplinary team operates a 24 hour, 7 day service, offering home-based assessment and treatment for people at risk of acute hospitalisation. As that team's success in preventing hospitalisation became apparent within the acute service, it was possible gradually to close acute beds. The locality now functions with 23 acute beds per 100,000 adult population. The money saved through bed closure was then released to fund a continuing service for those most in need. The PET team continues to act as gatekeeper to acute beds.

The Assertive Outreach Team offers intensive support to people with severe mental illness living across the locality. All clients are under the care of one consultant psychiatrist. The team uses qualified staff only. Each client is allocated a keyworker and a co-worker. Whilst the team operates a team approach to care, the keyworker takes a lead role, for example in coordinating reviews. The main aim of the team is to develop a therapeutic alliance with users of the service. Working out of hours in the evenings and at weekends means that the team is able to respond very quickly to changes in need. When clients are in crisis they would normally have been referred to the PET team, but the Assertive Outreach Team is increasingly able to manage crises within the team and provide home treatment.

4.4 The assertive outreach team

The team leader

The managerial arrangements for assertive outreach need careful consideration. The position of team leader is crucial to the success or failure of the service. The team leader needs to be in post for several months before the rest of the team to:

▷ negotiate the role of the assertive outreach team with other agencies, including convincing them of its value;

▷ identify potential clients for the service;

▷ recruit appropriate staff;

▷ provide and arrange training as staff come into post;

▷ find suitable premises;

▷ develop procedures – for example, for risk assessment and team supervision.

The team leader must be given a clear remit and sufficient authority. He or she must develop the vision of the service, both within the team and to outside agencies, by articulating the roles and responsibilities of the team in a clear operational policy. Too often, this Review has come across such policies which offer excellent vision and principles, but fall short on the detail. The client group must be precisely defined and identified. The operational policy must also establish the approach, specifying its long-term and intensive nature.

It is helpful if the team leader is a skilled professional who can provide an outreach service to a small number of users. In this way the team leader acts as a role model and demonstrates to outside agencies the type of work that can be done. Over time the team leader's role can be expected to change from setting up the assertive outreach service to developing the broader network of services that people need.

Creative tension with existing services

As assertive outreach staff come into post they will have to continue developing their working relationships with other services. A new service may be welcomed as an increase in resources, but staff in existing services can still feel wary and threatened. Initially this can lead to off-loading unsuitable or unpopular clients onto the new team, or sometimes staff in other services can refuse to refer clients to the new team.

There is a danger that a specialist service such as an assertive outreach team will be tempted to prove itself early on by accepting all comers, and thus lose its focus. The team will establish its reputation by demonstrating that its engagement work with individual users can lower the burden on other services. An assertive outreach service cannot start working with the whole of the identified client group overnight. It takes time to establish the new service with individual users and with other agencies.

New assertive outreach services do not operate in a vacuum. They take on responsibility for the care of a significant group of users. It is a key part of their role to negotiate specific packages of care with other providers. This can cause a knock-on effect in the system as a whole. Some degree of tension is therefore inevitable and healthy. Senior managers do, however, need to be prepared for this process and to ensure that these tensions can be discussed openly.

Team composition

Differences in experience, culture and social class can act as a barrier to effective working between client and mental health worker. Factors associated with the mental health problems of the user can also act as an impediment to engagement. Intrusive psychotic symptoms, depression and anxiety, deterioration of functioning and a decline in cognitive processes can generate feelings of suspicion, helplessness and hopelessness and reduce drive and motivation. These symptoms can make it exceptionally difficult for people to form relationships and to navigate the complex pathway to care.

The characteristics and style of mental health workers are crucial factors in successful engagement. The knowledge, skills and attitudes of the professional are also crucial. Unfortunately, much of the professional approach currently available to clients has its roots in outmoded hospital-based models of care. Training and education programmes bear little correlation with the needs of clients, modern service demands or the scientific evidence on effectiveness.

In developing teams which have the express purpose of engaging those high risk and vulnerable clients currently on the fringes of community care into an effective, needs-led system of social support, treatment and rehabilitation, the staff characteristics and skill-mix require careful consideration. Such teams would benefit from a multi-disciplinary mix of specialist mental health expertise and basic human qualities of good communication and sociability.

The range of tasks required of such teams to meet the social and health needs of clients, means that assertive outreach teams need to recruit staff beyond the traditional core mental health professions of psychiatry, psychology, occupational therapy, nursing and social work. Teams will often need to include so called non-professional staff or outreach workers. Outreach workers' expertise may lie outside the arena of formal qualifications but is no less valuable to the team in meeting the needs of clients.

Outreach workers

The Review used the term "outreach workers" to describe those workers in the assertive outreach teams who are not specialist mental health professionals. The desirable characteristics and qualities of a person employed as an outreach worker should be informed by the characteristics of the people who are difficult to engage in an area. One would expect a relatively high proportion to come from minority backgrounds or to have personal experience of mental health services.

The employment of people who have been service users in the past is similar to the employment of rehabilitated drug addicts in some addiction services. Positive experiences are reported in the US with the employment of service users as case managers,[108] and the increasing employment of service users as advocates in the UK is based on a similar philosophy. However, experience of being a service user is only one of several important characteristics, and should not be considered as essential in its own right or as a sufficient reason for inclusion in the team.

One of the primary roles of these workers will be to work alongside specialist mental health staff to facilitate engagement with users. This relationship can create the foundation on which to build a therapeutic programme of intervention and support. Outreach workers play another important role in engaging the client with other specialist mental health workers in the team. In this role, outreach workers will need to be able to work effectively as members of the multi-disciplinary team and achieve a cooperative relationship not only with service users but also with specialist mental health staff.

An additional role of the outreach worker is to facilitate the development of community support networks and develop further links with the multitude of services that clients need. They are also in a good position to monitor clients' mental states and wellbeing while helping them with a range of practical day-to-day issues.

Clearly, outreach workers will need considerable skills to carry out these functions. Training will also need to be provided in a range of areas including symptom and risk assessment skills.

Options for employing outreach workers

The Review has given some consideration to the best service model for employing outreach workers. A balance has to be struck between two contradictory demands.

On the one hand, outreach workers need to optimise their links with clients. Many members of this group resent statutory services for the reasons stated in Chapter 2. A group of outreach workers employed by the voluntary sector, supervised by experienced staff, might be considered to optimise the degree of engagement. Both the Tulip Outreach Team (described in **Box 5** earlier in this chapter) and the Elmore Community Support Team in Oxford are similar to such a model. The Review team visited the Elmore Team and some details of this service are given in **Box 7.**

Box 7. The Elmore Community Support Team

The Elmore Team is an independent provider based in Oxford and purchased by the statutory sector. The team is funded by the city council, the health authority, the social services department and the probation service.

The idea for the Elmore Team grew out of inter-agency work on difficult-to-place clients who were falling through the safety net of existing provision. The aim was to set up an independent team of peripatetic workers to support clients who were not engaging with services. The team was designed to promote inter-agency cooperation and encourage all relevant agencies to contribute to packages of care for difficult-to-place clients.

The team offers support to single adults with multiple needs who do not easily fit into existing provision and are not seen as the clear responsibility of any one agency. The team members see part of their function as "working through the chaos" without the need to rush to categorise clients who often have a confusing multiplicity of needs.

The Elmore Team service is based upon a pragmatic, needs-led approach. The service can be offered to someone going through a crisis, or over a long period of time. Team activities include helping to find and keep accommodation, helping with benefits, and with money management, and liaising with other supporting agencies.

The team has three support workers and one team coordinator, with backgrounds in social work, mental health nursing, homeless work and housing. There is a keyworking model and each team member has an individual caseload, but each team member also knows the other members' cases. Each support worker has about 15 active cases and about 10 cases requiring less input.

The total number of clients per annum is approximately 120 (with a further 100 rough sleepers who will not be worked with in such depth). The total cost of the team is about £160,000 per annum: this includes the cost of work with the rough sleepers.

On the other hand, although engagement is essential, it is only the first step of the process. Unless engagement leads to acceptance and receipt of services, care and interventions, little will have been achieved. A successful outcome seems most likely if outreach workers are employed by health or social services to work in an assertive outreach team. We are concerned about the extra boundary added if outreach workers are located in the voluntary sector. Boundaries already present many problems in the care of this group.

Reluctantly, we have come down on the side of employment by statutory services as the preferred option. However, there may be exceptions, for example, in areas where the voluntary sector is already strong and is accepted by statutory agencies as a valuable part of the spectrum of services. Equally, in patches where the statutory services have a particularly poor reputation with the local population, the voluntary sector may have greater success with the client group. In the end, what counts is the quality of all staff involved, their mutual support, and the willingness of services and agencies to cooperate.

Outreach workers could either be part of assertive outreach teams or could be members of CMHTs. In the latter case, they would need to have small and protected caseloads, and they could function by targeting the difficult-to-engage clients with long-term needs for intensive support. Their role would have some similarities to the role of community support worker, as described in a recent Sainsbury Centre report.[109]

Outreach workers will frequently be relatively inexperienced in mental health care, and turnover can be predicted to be fairly high. Particular attention should be given to screening outreach workers for their suitability, both in their ability to work responsibly with clients and their ability to liaise with professional staff. The limits of responsibility, especially considering risk, the lines of accountability, and the role of supervision need to be transparent. Outreach workers will require continuing training, and the design of a training programme is a priority, since no such course exists. Some of the best outreach workers may be keen to become nurses or social workers, and this should be encouraged by identifying options for career progression.

Characteristics of staff working with the client group

What follows is a list of the key attributes, skills and knowledge which will be required by all staff who work with the client group. This does not represent a rigorously evaluated set of criteria, but may be of help when local services are determining selection criteria when recruiting staff to specialist teams and services. Service providers should not be shy of including the personal characteristics which may underpin an ability to engage with the client group in the specifications, so long as these are applied fairly, showing regard for equal opportunities policies. This is an area in which knowledge is not sufficient to ensure effectiveness.

Some of the personal characteristics of staff who work successfully with this client group have been discussed earlier in this chapter. These points are summarised in **Box 8.**

Specific expertise required by staff working with the client group

Frequently mental health training and education is preoccupied with acute care and short-term treatments. Dealing with chronic mental illness is sometimes neglected. This tendency does not prepare staff for working with clients suffering from severe and enduring mental illness. Nor does it equip them with a framework for understanding the kind of knowledge, skills and attitudes necessary for working with longer term disability and handicap.

Box 8. Personal characteristics of staff working with the client group

- ▶ Specialist mental health staff and outreach workers must be **needs-led** in their approach and allow the users' priorities to set the agenda.

- ▶ Staff need to have the right **style** for the clients they are engaging; it may help if they come from a similar ethnic group or have had experience of using mental health services.

- ▶ Staff need to be able to work with users in **informal settings.**

- ▶ People with **low Expressed Emotion** seem to be particularly successful at working with the client group.

- ▶ Staff need to have **realistic expectations** about the scope for improvement in clients' lives and to be committed to long-term therapeutic relationships.

Table 3. Expertise and knowledge required in assertive outreach teams

Assessment and planning skills:	Needs assessment Care planning and care management Mental state assessment Risk assessment Functional assessment
Service coordination:	Finding housing Claiming welfare benefits Finding work opportunities Accessing physical healthcare
Direct work with clients and families:	Medication management Monitoring side-effects of medication Psychological aspects of treatment adherence Behaviour management Problem-solving and goal-setting Crisis intervention Working with people with dual diagnosis Working with families Counselling Advocacy Providing information and education
Team-working and good practice:	Multi-disciplinary team-working Anti-discriminatory practice Confidentiality

In addition to the personal characteristics listed above, assertive outreach teams need access to special expertise and knowledge in a variety of areas. These are summarised in **Table 3.**

Formal treatment interventions

Some members of teams will need expertise in formal treatment interventions. This is reflected in the section on direct work with clients in **Table 3.**

In recent years there have been important developments in the range of interventions which have proven effectiveness in the treatment of severe mental illnesses such as schizophrenia.[110]

▷ Medication

Over the last few years several new anti-psychotic and anti-depressant drugs have emerged. They promise greater effectiveness and fewer side-effects, which may be of particular importance to the Review client group. The higher cost of the new medications is a reason to be cautious about replacing older and well-known drugs, but for the Review group, with its intensive service use, the argument of added cost seems inappropriate. Indeed, indications that such medication should be used may help to identify and prioritise members of the client group.

▷ Crisis intervention

The effectiveness of providing community-based, acute care alternatives to hospitalisation – such as a crisis team – has been well demonstrated.[111,112]

▷ Behavioural family interventions

Although many of the Review group live alone, others either live with, or are in regular contact with, family or carers. There is now compelling evidence to support the effectiveness of behavioural family interventions in the management of schizophrenia. This approach involves several components, including provision of education and information about the illness, promotion of medication adherence, stress management and problem-solving, and managing difficult problem behaviours.[113] Expected outcomes from this approach include reduction in relapse rates, improved social and clinical functioning, and high rates of user and carer satisfaction.

▷ Treatment adherence training

Recent developments in the area of motivational development and promoting adherence to treatment, including medication, look very promising. A number of techniques – including Cognitive Behaviour Therapy, problem-solving, and motivational interviewing – increase cooperation with drug therapy and improve global functioning.[114]

▷ Early warning signs and early intervention

Emerging research has highlighted the corrosive nature of regular psychotic episodes and suggests that poor long-term outcome is linked to the frequency and intensity of such breakdowns. This approach, pioneered in the UK and Australia, involves training users and carers in the early detection of signs of relapse and organising rapid intervention to prevent or ameliorate the severity of the episode.[115]

▷ Specific psychological interventions

Cognitive and behavioural approaches have been used in various forms in attempts to ameliorate aspects of schizophrenia such as persisting hallucinations and delusions. While success has been variable and the results are still preliminary, some of the findings appear promising. Interventions have included attempts to modify the personal involvement surrounding the symptoms, and to lessen the anxiety, concern and conviction associated with the experience rather than attempting to eliminate the symptoms directly.[116,117]

We would not expect that all practitioners in the team should be competent in all these interventions. Part of the role of members of the team would be to negotiate access to these treatments as appropriate. However, some members of the team should certainly have some of the skills outlined above.

Relying on drugs and hospital beds for the treatment of people with severe mental illness should no longer be, and mostly is not, accepted as good practice. As exclusive interventions, these are no longer socially or clinically acceptable options. The new approaches must offer comprehensive social care packages as well as access to effective interventions delivered across a range of settings.

Work with people with dual diagnosis

As suggested above, teams need to have a system for working with people with a dual diagnosis of mental illness and substance misuse. Some of the barriers to such work were discussed in **Chapter 2.** In the US there has been considerable research on developing services for people with dual diagnosis. Whilst there are methodological problems with some of the evaluations of these services, there is some evidence that services have been developed which improve outcomes for people with dual diagnosis. The essential features of services which seem to work well in the US are summarised in **Box 9** and may be of interest in looking at the options for service development in this area. It needs to be remembered, however, that what might work well in the US may not necessarily be easily translated to the UK and further service evaluation needs to be undertaken of UK services.

Box 9. US experience of providing services for people with dual diagnosis[118]

▶ Services integrate interventions for substance misuse and psychosis so that the same keyworker or case manager has time, training, and resources to do both forms of work.

▶ Conventional substance misuse interventions are adapted to make them more appropriate for people who have a major mental illness so that there is (a) greater tolerance of relapse and people are not ejected from services because they fail to achieve or maintain abstinence; (b) greater emphasis on developing social skills and problem-solving methods which allow people to negotiate difficult social situations without using drugs and alcohol.

▶ Services make less use of high Expressed Emotion techniques such as group sessions in which people are very challenging to each other: these can be disturbing to people with schizophrenia and may sometimes bring on a relapse.

▶ Unlike some substance misuse services, services for people with dual diagnosis can continue to encourage the use of psychotropic medication.

▶ The emphasis is on trying to increase motivation and being practical and supportive rather than challenging and exploratory; there is also a strong emphasis on helping people develop social networks and activities which do not involve substance misuse.

▶ Caseloads are small, staff receive a high level of training, supervision and support, and the general approach is an assertive outreach model.

Conclusion

We have set out in some detail our reasons for concluding that assertive outreach is one of the essential services for the client group, and given some guidance on implementation. In Chapter 5, we outline a number of other, equally important, services which need to be available. Assertive outreach teams will not succeed without a suitable range of services with which to engage their clients.

CHAPTER

Essential services: accommodation, daytime activity and welfare advice

This chapter:

▷ continues the description of essential services for the client group and focuses on accommodation, daytime activity and welfare advice;

▷ draws some preliminary conclusions about what sort of services may offer best value for money.

5.1 Residential provision and housing

One of the most important service components for this client group is the provision of stable and friendly accommodation with adequate support. Clearly, there is no single model which will be able to address the variety of individual needs and preferences found in this target group. Age, gender, culture and past experiences will all determine clients' preferences.

There is some evidence that intensively staffed, high supervision options such as 24 hour nursed care may be effective in improving social outcomes and adherence to medication, and providing rapid response in a crisis. They may also increase user satisfaction compared with traditional alternatives, such as hospital. Even so, they are often unpopular with users themselves.[119]

The evidence on factors determining acceptability to users suggests that privacy, autonomy, and help with the practicalities of money and bills are much more important than professional support and medication. Many members of this group are likely to prefer independent flats or bed-sits, albeit with intensive community support, rather than the group-living option in traditional supported hostels.

The Review identified two main accommodation options for the client group:

▷ ordinary housing with intensive support;

▷ 24 hour nursed care.

Ordinary housing with intensive support

The Review team visited the Dispersed Intensively Supported Housing Scheme (DISH) in Nottingham, which is described in **Box 10** and seems well worth consideration. It combines independent housing – which is cost-effective and meets users' aspirations – with a high level of flexible and skilled NHS staff support.

While the Nottingham scheme is a useful model, it is possible to postulate similar models. For example, sheltered wardened accommodation with independent flatlets, or a network of small group homes with intensive support, might provide a similar mix of independence and support.

These types of models rely for their success on a number of factors including:

▷ ready access to inpatient care or staffed units if required;

▷ a large enough client-base to justify a scheme;

▷ concentration of the homes in a reasonably small geographic area to allow peripatetic staff to access clients quickly and easily;

▷ appropriate selection of clients to ensure that they are capable of supported independent living, but equally that they require a higher level of support than that delivered by a generic CMHT;

▷ a sufficient degree of community acceptance.

Such schemes will only be appropriate and viable in areas where:

▷ the Health Authority is able to invest sufficient resources to ensure that the scheme stands as part of a more comprehensive package of services; in

Box 10. The Nottingham Dispersed Intensively Supported Housing Scheme

The Nottingham Dispersed Intensively Supported Housing Scheme (DISH) was established in 1990 for long-stay patients who had been discharged from the Mapperley and Saxendale hospitals, but for whom neither a residential facility nor traditional community psychiatric services were appropriate.

Current referrals are from a newer group of younger long-stay patients. Most patients are aged between 18 and 40. They tend to have a history of mental illness but to have had limited inpatient stays. Many have become revolving door patients and have a history of offending and compulsory admissions.

DISH is targeted at people with an enduring mental health problem and high support needs who would otherwise need to be accommodated in residential care. The scheme provides intensive support to clients in their own homes. Clients are only accepted by DISH if they are assessed as needing at least three visits per week, although daily or twice daily visits can be made if required.

DISH is made up of four teams of eight or nine workers, and the ceiling on the number of clients is 63 for the service, or 15/16 clients per team. The service operates seven days per week from 9.00am-9.00pm. There is an out-of-hours telephone support service provided by night staff at a community-based residential unit. These staff can refer clients to senior staff within DISH. Each client has a keyworker, but there is also a team approach to care, so that a client can receive care from anyone in the team.

Just over 50% of clients live in accommodation which is provided as part of the DISH scheme and owned by a number of housing associations. Other clients live in council properties, or their own homes. Most clients have a tenancy agreement with their housing association or the city council and can give one month's notice. The accommodation becomes the permanent home of the client as long as it continues to meet their needs and wishes. If a client leaves DISH, he or she can continue the tenancy and the housing association will try to provide a replacement property for DISH.

The philosophy behind the DISH scheme includes focusing on the clients' strengths, interests and abilities and not upon their weaknesses, deficits and pathology. Clients are encouraged to use community facilities rather than segregated mental health services. Engagement with the clients has been greatly helped by the fact that DISH is offering accommodation and very intensive input. Even some difficult-to-engage clients who have presented major problems in other services have done well in DISH. If a DISH client presents a risk of dangerousness the client is moved to an appropriate form of care.

The revenue cost of the 63 clients is £750,000 per annum or £10 – 12,000 per client per annum excluding housing costs.

Nottingham this has been achieved by the reinvestment of monies previously locked up in a Victorian asylum;

▷ there is a concentration of clients requiring the service; this is unlikely outside large towns or cities;

▷ the community is sufficiently accepting towards clients for the scheme to be workable; this may not be true in a few inner city and suburban areas;

▷ links with housing and social services are good enough to ensure that the scheme can be implemented and sustained.

In areas where these requirements can be met, it would appear that this type of scheme has a major role to play in supporting the client group.

24 hour nursed care

In examining the viability of this option for the client group, the Review endorsed the potential of 24 hour nursed accommodation to:

▷ offer appropriate care for people who need the continual support of skilled staff to cope with daily life and whose behaviour may require frequent monitoring for risk of harm either to themselves or others;

▷ be a useful transitional step for people who have become institutionalised by long periods in hospital or prison, or who need to redevelop their independent living skills after long periods of sleeping rough;[120]

▷ provide an acceptable alternative to long-stay hospital back wards or secure accommodation where a high level of security is not justified.

However, 24 hour nursed care does also have some important disadvantages for the client group:

▷ the lifestyles of some clients are too chaotic to tolerate the environment;

▷ 24 hour nursed care is not popular with some service-users; a survey of users considered by clinicians to be in need of 24 hour nursed care showed that their preferred living arrangement was an independent flat with psychiatric staff visiting;[121]

▷ 24 hour nursed care is expensive; its rapid expansion could only be achieved through a capital-led initiative which runs the danger of tying up mental health resources in an inflexible way.

There may be two sub-groups who will particularly require this form of care. Firstly, it is appropriate for people who:

▷ have significant histories of risk to themselves and others;

▷ have continuing active symptoms despite medication;

▷ relapse very rapidly if medication is discontinued or the environment is stressful.

As it is an expensive option, (up to a maximum of £50,000 per year or around £1m for twenty years' care) it is essential that the sub-group requiring it is clearly identified as such and that an individual's progress and preferences are kept under regular review. Undoubtedly clients requiring a home for life in such accommodation do exist in very small numbers and it would be wrong to suggest otherwise.

Secondly, there are people who may require 24 hour nursed care for a limited period as part of a rehabilitation programme. This might take place over a period of say, three years, after which the client would move into less heavily supported accommodation. This sort of treatment plan is likely to make the setting more acceptable to clients and might provide better value from this high-cost intervention.

Like DISH, and assertive outreach teams, 24 hour nursed accommodation is likely to be most relevant to districts with larger numbers of clients requiring high levels of support and is likely to be most effective as part of a spectrum of services. Where such a spectrum is absent, there is a danger that this form of care may be used as a substitute for other more cost-effective services which have not yet been developed. A danger with this type of expensive capital-led type of provision is that it can lock services into models that are costly but not necessarily effective. Assertive outreach services and intensive residential care options have striking potential to add value to

Box 11. Mental Health Services of Salford NHS Trust

Salford mental health services have been designed to offer a series of tiers of care according to the need for security or supervision. This includes the standard access to high security and medium secure services at the top of the pyramid, and to inpatient care, community care and primary care at the lower end of the pyramid. Particular attention has been paid to developing a good range of options between inpatient care and secure care for clients who have a long-term need for high support. These options include:

▶ a community-based hostel ward providing 24 hour nursed care (12 places);

▶ an on-site hospital-based hostel ward providing 24 hour nursed care for younger clients with enduring mental health needs, some of whom may have previously required provision of care in secure or semi-secure environments (10 places);

▶ a high dependency unit providing semi-secure care for clients who need a highly supported environment and cannot be supported in 24 hour nursed care, but who do not need medium secure care (15 places).

The impetus to provide 24 hour nursed care in a community-based hostel ward came from bed-blocking in the acute admissions unit by a group of new long-stay patients. The average age of the hostel clients is 35 and they tend to have a severe psychosis. This is often combined with a history of violence, reluctance to take psychotropic medication, and problems with substance misuse. The clients require a safe and stable environment and help with daily living. The hostel provides daily monitoring of clients' mental state and skilled management of challenging behaviour. Residents of the hostel are encouraged to use community facilities whenever possible.

Residents can be detained under the Mental Health Act 1983, and between one-third and one-half of the clients are detained. This is usually because non-compliance with medication and lack of help-seeking behaviour increase the risk of dangerousness, or because the level of illness is such that intensive and continuing care is needed.

The average length of stay is two years, although some clients will stay permanently. Some will move on to more independent living and there are many links with the local voluntary housing sector.

each other. This underlines the importance of considering service components for this client group as part of a system, rather than in isolation.

The Review team visited the Mental Health Services of Salford NHS Trust where 24 hour nursed care is offered as part of a good spectrum of services. Some details of the service are given in **Box 11.**

As set out in **Table 1** in **Chapter 4,** a number of other accommodation options should be considered for the client group as local circumstances dictate. For example, the Review team visited Thames Reach Housing Association, and was impressed by its provision of self-contained flats for mentally ill people who have been street homeless in central London. Some details of this service are given in **Box 12.**

Box 12. Thames Reach Housing Association: self-contained flats with high support

Thames Reach provides two housing projects as part of the Homeless Mentally Ill Initiative, each containing self-contained flats, staff facilities and shared recreational and laundry facilities. One project also incorporates a small hostel. Thames Reach aims to provide temporary accommodation with support, and access to permanent rehousing.

The initiative is targeted at people with chaotic lifestyles and multiple needs who require high levels of support but are often resistant to any form of engagement or therapeutic intervention. The projects have been successful in settling people into temporary accommodation, but the lack of permanent high-support housing options has made resettlement difficult.

Many residents have previously been evicted from shared accommodation but have had difficulty in securing the accommodation of their choice because of their disruptive behaviour. The projects have been designed sensitively, so that tenants have privacy and opportunities for autonomy, but at the same time there is a high level of staff support, including on-call support in emergencies.

The projects are staffed by experienced but non-specialist workers who use the keyworker approach. Many of the residents have resisted engagement with mainstream services so that there is a heavy reliance on the project staff to identify individual problems and needs and to take steps to meet those needs. A specialist mental health team provides support to the project, both to the staff group and individual residents. Effective joint working procedures are essential to ensure that the needs of such a challenging client group can be met.

5.2 Daytime activities

The direct and indirect evidence for the effectiveness of work in improving long-term outcomes for people with severe mental illness is now very strong.[122] Structured activity is clearly a useful form of therapy in itself, and, particularly for this target group, the value of offering an alternative to the role of being a patient is of fundamental importance. For many people, the idea that they are moving towards meaningful occupation may be almost as powerful a motivation as securing employment itself. It will certainly be one of the main determinants of successful engagement. Services which cannot offer at least some hope in this area will struggle to involve this sceptical, and generally alienated, user group.

Although the findings regarding the general importance of work and occupation are very strong, the evidence comparing the outcomes of different kinds of schemes – sheltered social firms and cooperatives, placement and job coach models, or user-led businesses – is relatively weak.

Different models are needed to suit users with different levels of ability and different ambitions. Some users may wish to achieve complete social reintegration, as opposed to partial integration in segregated schemes such as user-run cooperatives.

The image of work schemes is central in determining the amount of social and psychological benefit associated with attendance and hence is central in determining acceptability to users.[123] The other factor which affects acceptability is the level of financial remuneration. This is of particular importance for this group with its high proportion of younger people. Despite the intention signalled by the Government's

Welfare to Work proposals, it is still unclear how much flexibility will be introduced into the benefits system to help people move more easily across the boundary between disability and economic productivity.

The Disability Working Allowance, which represented an attempt to introduce some flexibility, has had a notoriously low take-up (estimated at less than 1% of those eligible) and only offers means-tested support for a very short period of time trying out a new job (8 weeks). The person then risks returning to a much lower rate of benefit if they find they cannot cope in open employment.

As an alternative, the All Party Parliamentary Mental Health Group recommended a rehabilitation allowance which would not be means-tested. The allowance would follow the claimant into employment and provide a safeguard if the claimant needed to return to benefits.[124] Others have suggested increasing the earnings disregard and introducing greater flexibility about what can constitute therapeutic work.

Whatever the mechanism, the financial rewards (and in some instances the penalties) of participation in work programmes will be crucial in determining whether users engage with, and benefit from, work rehabilitation services.

Box 13 gives four examples of schemes to provide daytime opportunities for people with long-term mental health problems.

Box 13. Examples of schemes to provide daytime opportunities

The following examples are drawn from a report by the Sainsbury Centre for Mental Health.[125]

Hillside House was set up in 1990 by St Mungo's Association and was the first Clubhouse to be established in Britain. Clubhouses function as both clubs and workplaces. The members are people with long-term mental health problems who run the Clubhouse with the staff. Through their involvement in the work and social life of the Clubhouse, members may develop the confidence to move on into transitional employment. In transitional employment, members work in ordinary employment with support from the Clubhouse and at normal rates of pay.

The **Hanley Road Resource Centre** was opened in 1991 for people who were being resettled from a large psychiatric hospital. The aims were to enable the users to access ordinary social and leisure facilities and become more integrated into the local community, and to involve them in part-time paid work at the Centre, including taking a part in its running.

The **Feathers Place Project** was established in 1989 to provide work opportunities for people disadvantaged by illness or disability, particularly those with mental health problems. It is a limited liability company, selling high quality goods and services to the general public, and relies on its commercial income to meet a substantial part of the total running costs. It is almost entirely staffed and managed by the workforce, most of whom have long-term mental health problems.

The **Blackthorn Garden Project** was set up in 1991 to provide a work environment in the community for people with long-term mental health problems. The aim was to establish a garden, bakery and cafe. The project aimed to create work and social situations in which people of different abilities and backgrounds (healthy and ill) could mix together.

5.3 Welfare advice

Mental health workers may often find that welfare advice is one of the main ways in which they can help clients. This can be of particular importance with clients who are difficult-to-engage and suspicious of services, as it provides a good incentive for engagement. Mental health workers may not have the expertise required, however, to help their clients negotiate the benefits system and deal with the paperwork.

A number of approaches can be taken to tackling these issues:

▷ individual members of generic or specialist mental health teams can develop welfare advice as an area of expertise; they can then act as a resource for team clients, or for other team members;

▷ team members can facilitate access to mainstream services such as Citizens' Advice Bureaux;

▷ specialist welfare advice services can be established;

▷ an experienced welfare benefits worker can undertake sessional work in the assertive outreach team. In areas of lesser morbidity, it is equally important to secure regular input from sessional workers to the CMHT or other teams. The use of the Lisson Grove welfare benefits package by clinical teams has been documented,[126] and a brief description of one such service which operates in London is given in **Box 14.**

5.4 The economics of the service responses

It is clear that a range of options for the client group has been developed nationally and internationally. It is less clear which of these offer best value for money. Little hard evidence currently exists about this, but it will be an important question to address both to obtain investment in services for the group in the first place, and in order to maximise the outputs and outcomes from that investment.

Box 14. A specialist welfare service

The Bethlem and Maudsley NHS Trust operates a welfare service for in-patients five days per week. A drop in service is provided for two hours on 4 days and staff make ward visits and arrange individual appointments at other times. The aim is to maximise benefit entitlement and provide an information service for keyworkers.

The service used to extend to community teams but this proved difficult to fund. However, funding has been prioritised from within two of the sector teams and welfare advice has been re-established for 15 hours per week. The service provided by the advice workers at the community team bases offers pre-arranged appointments and a drop-in

facility providing assistance with completion of specialised benefit applications such as Disability Living Allowance.

A combination of coordinating skills, sensitivity to the applicants' needs, close liaison with the community team and an in-depth understanding of the benefit system is essential to achieving a successful claim.

The backgrounds of the advice workers are very mixed. Some have Citizens' Advice Bureau or legal experience; others have a background in working with relevant client groups. Training in welfare rights is provided through formal training and on-the-job experience.

In order at least to obtain some information, to open up lines of inquiry, and to illustrate some of the issues, an economic analysis was carried out based on six patient care pathways. These were either based on real but simplified patient histories, or on professionals' experience of real care pathways. They are illustrated in **Diagram 2,** and supporting details are contained in **Appendix 7.** They can be summarised as follows using non-London prices:

1 A year in 24 hour nursed care costs £36,000.

2 A year in dispersed intensively supported housing with a three week hospital stay would cost £20,000.

3 One year of support in the community with assertive outreach, including six weeks' inpatient care, costs £12,000.

4 Care for "Peter" over one year – a simplification of a real case of someone apparently poorly managed within the community who then offended – cost £28,000.

5 Care over one year for a revolving door patient who did not offend cost £25,000.

6 An alternative, less complex revolving door package cost £17,000 over one year.

Clearly much more work needs to be done with costing specific interventions and real care pathways before clear conclusions can be reached about value for money. However, some *prima facie* conclusions might be:

▷ 24 hour nursed care is expensive and therefore should be limited to those with a clear clinical need for this service;

▷ managing very needy patients inappropriately is probably more expensive than managing them well;

▷ the price range for assertive outreach plus various forms of supported housing may be £10-25,000. This is costly, but cheaper than 24 hour nursed care and within about the same range as, or less than, the costs incurred by revolving door patients.

Conclusion

Table 1 in Chapter 4 set out the range of services required by the client group. In Chapters 4 and 5 we have identified the service functions which we regard as central to an effective service response to this group: assertive outreach; suitable accommodation; daytime activity; and welfare advice. In Chapter 6 we outline the fundamental requirements for change and suggest six basic steps to meeting the group's needs.

DIAGRAM 2: PATHWAYS OF CARE: DIFFERENT COSTS

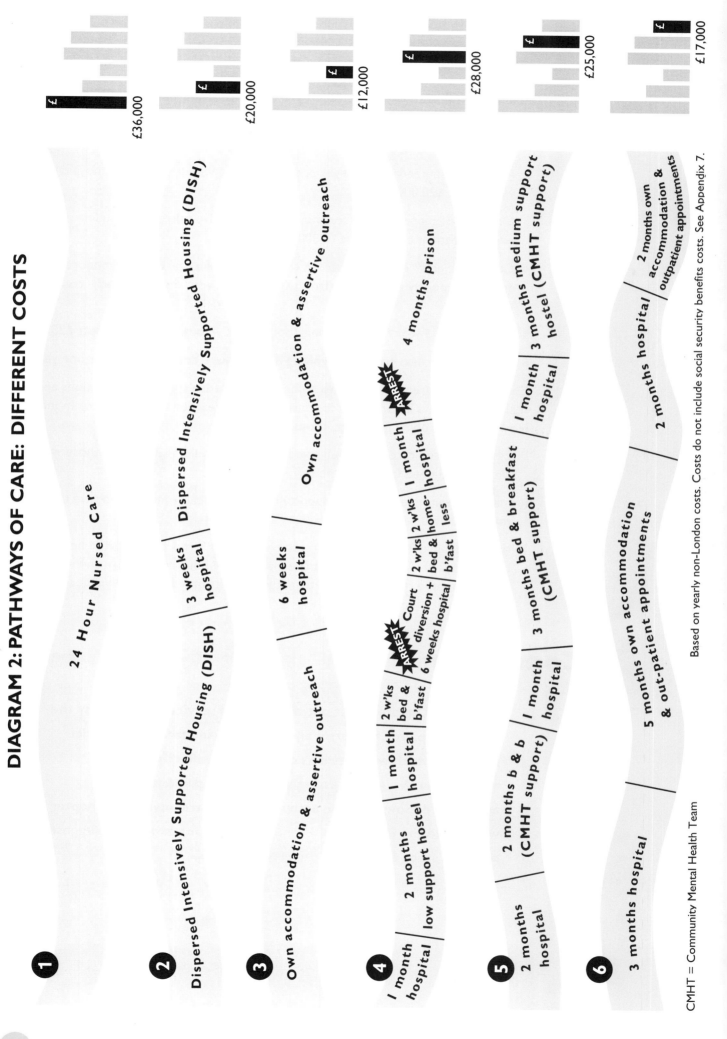

1 24 Hour Nursed Care — £36,000

2 Dispersed Intensively Supported Housing (DISH) | 3 weeks hospital | Dispersed Intensively Supported Housing (DISH) — £20,000

3 Own accommodation & assertive outreach | 6 weeks hospital | Own accommodation & assertive outreach — £12,000

4 1 month hospital | 2 months low support hostel | 1 month hospital | 2 w'ks bed & b'fast | **ARREST** Court diversion + 6 weeks hospital | 2 w'ks bed & b'fast | 1 month hospital | 2 w'ks bed & home-less | **ARREST** 4 months prison — £28,000

5 2 months hospital | 2 months b & b (CMHT support) | 1 month hospital | 3 months bed & breakfast (CMHT support) | 1 month hospital | 3 months medium support hostel (CMHT support) — £25,000

6 3 months hospital | 5 months own accommodation & out-patient appointments | 2 months hospital | 2 months own accommodation & outpatient appointments — £17,000

CMHT = Community Mental Health Team

Based on yearly non-London costs. Costs do not include social security benefits costs. See Appendix 7.

CHAPTER 6

The next steps

This chapter:

▷ sets out six basic steps to meeting the client group's needs;

▷ identifies the national policy requirements to support these steps;

▷ suggests areas where further research and development are needed.

It is clear that some services work better for the client group for this Review than others and that some may offer better value for money, although there is a need for more rigorous economic analysis. The basic service model which emerges is one of:

▷ **assertive outreach** strongly linked to the full range of health and social care provision;

▷ meaningful **daytime activity**;

▷ **supported accommodation**, with access to residential options and hospital when required.

In some areas, services are well on the way to providing this core range of functions, although the labels applied to the services and to the client group may differ. Others have a long way to go. If the needs of the group are to be met across the country as a whole a commitment to targeted inter-agency working is required both nationally and locally.

6.1 Six steps to meeting the group's needs

The Review has identified six fundamental building blocks which must be in place locally to deliver change:

1 A **strategic approach** is required locally involving all the key agencies.

2 **Assertive outreach** must be in place within each area. This will usually be provided by a bespoke team when the client-base is big enough.

3 A **human resource plan** is required to provide and equip staff to deliver assertive outreach.

4 Assertive outreach teams must be **effectively managed**.

5 A **range of provision** is required locally for assertive outreach to draw on.

6 Providers need to establish adequate **information systems** to support assertive outreach.

National policy requirements

To support this, national policy development will be required, with the aim of facilitating and driving forward local activity. It will need to focus on the following key areas:

▷ inter-agency working;

▷ finance;

▷ human resources;

▷ performance management of service development;

▷ development and implementation of a national R&D strategy.

Further details of the six basic steps are given in the following sections.

1 Local strategy development

The needs of the client group cannot be met without multi-agency, coordinated service delivery. While much can be achieved by staff linking individual clients to generic services, a strategic framework and strong leadership is required to put in place a range of interrelated services.

Clearly, it is important to avoid bureaucracy, but it is hard to see how progress will be made without some formal meetings. The Review concluded that Health Authorities should have the lead responsibility for establishing inter-agency strategy groups within their areas to address the needs of the group. A list of local agencies with an interest in the client group is set out in **Box 15.**

Not all these agencies and stakeholders will need to be on the strategy group in all areas, but most will need to be involved. **Diagram 3** contains a schematic representation of how the group will draw on local agencies and the lines of accountability. There will be some local variation, and change over time as the NHS White Paper is implemented, but the basic principles will be unchanged.

The initial tasks to be undertaken by the strategy group, roughly in chronological order, are:

▷ to agree an **operational definition** of the client group requiring assertive outreach within the local area. This could be based on current definitions of severe mental illness (such as those suggested by the Department of Health in *Building Bridges*) and the specific factors which define this group as discussed in Chapters 1 and 2 above;

▷ to commission a **needs assessment** for the group. This could be coordinated by the public health department in the Health Authority, or the mental health Trust working with social services and housing authorities and the other stakeholders. In many areas mental health Trusts should be able to identify the majority of individuals. It is essential that the assessment is based upon actual numbers of clients as well as upon public health information. An assessment will be needed of the most pressing needs faced by the client group within the area – these will vary across the country, but each of the factors described in Chapters 4 and 5 should be addressed;

▷ to **benchmark existing services** against the needs assessment and against the basket of required services described in this report and in central guidance;

Box 15. Key stakeholders

▶ Health Authorities

▶ NHS Trusts

▶ Primary health care

▶ Social Services Authorities

▶ Social care providers

▶ Employers

▶ Employment Rehabilitation Officers

▶ Housing Authorities

▶ Housing Associations

▶ Police

▶ Probation Service

▶ Social Security local offices

▶ Voluntary sector

▶ Users' groups

▶ Carers' organisations

DIAGRAM 3: STRUCTURE AND OPERATION OF THE INTER-AGENCY STRATEGY GROUP

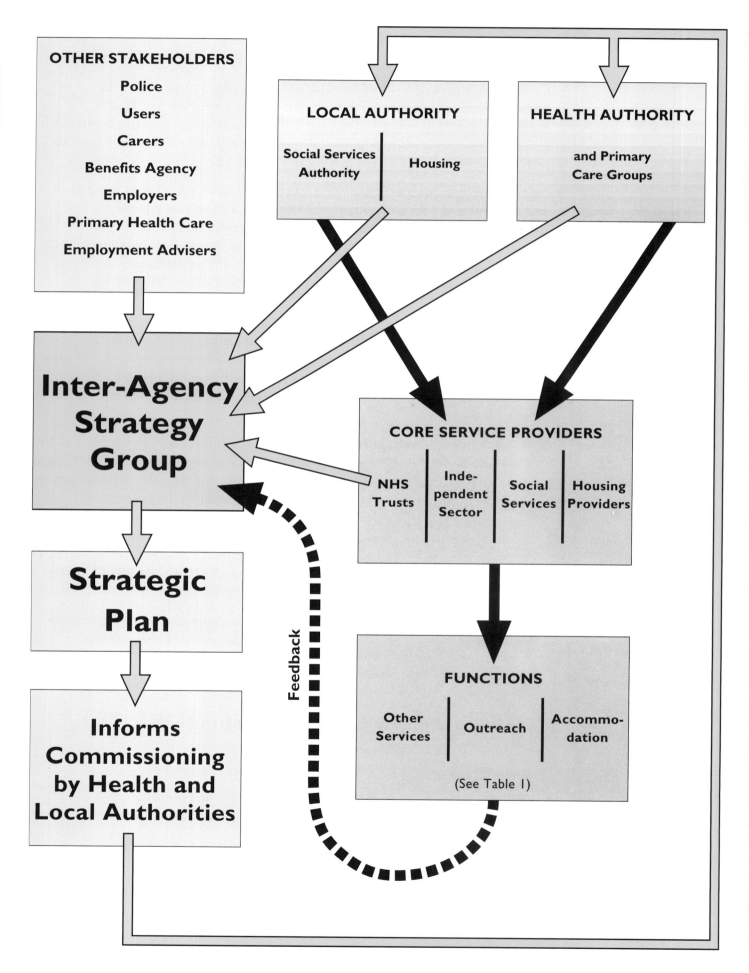

▷ to **prepare a plan** for developing and sustaining services which can meet the needs of the group. This can be published separately or as a part of community care or mental health service strategic plans. The plan needs to clarify local responsibility for each aspect of service provision required by the group. It also needs to set out which of those services are already in place and which require further development. This broad agreement will then enable teams to negotiate more detailed service level agreements once assertive outreach is up and running;

▷ as part of the plan there will need to be a **human resource strategy** which includes refined criteria for selecting staff to deliver assertive outreach and other services. Some suggestions for the necessary competencies were made in Chapter 4. The human resource strategy also needs to set out training strategies, which should be developed using shared and joint training wherever possible. This issue is covered in more detail below.

2 Development of assertive outreach

This is the core task, and is addressed in considerable detail in **Chapter 4.**

3 The development and implementation of a human resource plan

Having the right staff with the right skills in place is fundamental to the successful delivery of assertive outreach and other services required by the client group. This is primarily a management issue requiring:

▷ the best possible match between the clients' needs and the workers' skills;

▷ accurate targeting of services so that the highly trained professionals within the team concentrate on the job for which they were trained, rather than attempting to fill a gap in services which can best be provided by workers without formal qualifications.

Having defined the client group to be targeted by assertive outreach and the overall plan for service development, detailed selection criteria for staff can be established. These can be refined in the light of experience and service evaluation.

As discussed in Chapter 4, it is likely that some of the skills and characteristics needed for working with the group relate to the personal characteristics of the workers and cannot be inculcated through training. On the other hand, many of the skills required by staff do not fall into this category, and training will be key to establishing and maintaining the proper functioning of the team as well as personal development and morale. Some areas of training, such as confidentiality and risk management, must be undertaken by all staff. Others can be areas of specialism for individual team members.

Training should form part of a continuous staff development programme linked systematically with appraisal and business planning cycles. Team members should receive professional supervision (say one day a month) in which an experienced practitioner helps them develop their skills, focusing on the realities of practice. This will often be more valuable than external training courses.

Steps which individual service providers (including independent sector providers) will need to take include:

▷ developing local competency frameworks;

▷ developing or accessing the necessary spread of training opportunities, preferably in concert with other local agencies;

▷ implementing or refining personal development plans as part of the appraisal process and business planning cycle;

▷ setting aside time and resources to enable staff to fulfil their personal development plans; team leaders should be accountable for ensuring that members are enabled to complete their personal development plans.

4 Effective management

Much has been written about effective team management both in the generic management literature and in relation to CMHTs.[127] There is evidence that good management is the single most important factor in allowing teams to function and maintain morale, even when workloads are high. It is hard therefore to place too much emphasis on this factor.

This report is not the place for a detailed review of the literature on team management, but the following principles are of particular importance in managing assertive outreach teams or any services incorporating an assertive outreach function:

▷ **Team members must be clear about their roles**: good quality, objective- and function-based job descriptions are required. Clarity about the aims of the team should allow clarity about individual roles, responsibilities and accountability. A distinction needs to be made about what is core to all team members and what is specific to each individual member of staff. This is similar to the issues raised in a recent review of multi-disciplinary training.[128]

▷ **Caseload and case-mix must be managed**: team members should be clear about the maximum caseload they will be expected to carry and managers must monitor this. It is also essential to develop clear targeting criteria and for the team manager to monitor the team's adherence to those criteria.

▷ **Staff support** needs to be addressed through individual and group sessions to manage stress and negative feelings.

▷ The team manager should be **trained in management**, regardless of his or her professional background, and competent to manage staff of differing backgrounds working under pressure.

▷ The team manager must be **visible** and must be **accountable** for the overall performance of the team. The leader must be willing to lead from the front, especially when something goes wrong.

▷ The team manager must be familiar with issues such as **risk management, inter-agency working, record keeping and information systems** and be capable of setting up, communicating and managing realistic procedures in these areas.

5 Providing a range of services locally

It is easy enough to state the range of services to which members of the client group will from time to time require access, but less easy to ensure that they are all in place locally. **Table 1** in **Chapter 4** contains a list of the elements which may be required to support the client group. Exactly what is required locally will depend on the size and case-mix within the client group, as discussed in Chapter 4.

One of the core functions of the inter-agency strategy group must be to plan the range of services which the client group will need to access with support from assertive outreach or community mental health team members.

6 Information systems

It will be difficult for team members and partner agencies to manage individuals' care without an adequate information system. This will underpin needs assessment, audit, case reviews, and service development. A separate stand-alone system for the current client group is to be avoided: systems should be built around CPA registers or local case registers.

6.2 The national policy requirements

If services for this group are to be developed in an effective way nationally, a clearer policy focus is required. Policy development should aim to support, facilitate and underpin the local development of assertive outreach, and the establishment of the required range of services.

The essential elements of a coherent policy to support service development for the group are discussed below.

1 Action to encourage inter-agency working

The new Government has recognised the vital importance of alliance-building and inter-agency working to deliver continuing care across a range of client groups. It is committed to implementing a range of incentives to closer working including allowing budget-pooling. The Sainsbury Centre will be publishing a separate report on this issue shortly and has already published a range of proposals for moving matters forward.[129]

Such initiatives have clear potential in relation to the current client group. At present the division of budgets between secondary health care, primary health care, social care and housing gives each agency an incentive for clients to be cared for in a different part of the system, rather than to work together to maximise the efficiency of the total available funds.

At operational level there might be significant benefits from outreach teams holding unified budgets for the client group and using a care management model to plan individual care packages. This type of approach could usefully be piloted.

Coupled with the policy initiatives already promised on inter-agency working, there is a need for strong performance management by Regional Offices of the various agencies involved with the care of this group. Regional Offices should require to see and sign off strategic service plans from within their regions and use national benchmarks as to their adequacy.

This will require much closer working between Government Departments, particularly the Department of Health, the Department of the Environment, Transport and the Regions and the Department for Education and Employment. Without a clear lead and example from the centre, it is hard to expect local agencies to work closely together. This cooperation between Departments should be reflected in:

▷ regular meetings to agree strategies in relation to mental health;

▷ where appropriate, the issue of joint guidance;

▷ joint developmental initiatives.

One key problem in working across boundaries is that the planning cycle for housing is different to that for health and social services. The majority of funding for housing development comes through Housing Investment Project Bids. The planning cycle for these bids begins in July and August, whereas health and social services start their planning cycle in the Autumn. This creates difficulties in cross-boundary working, both for the current client group, and for a range of others. The Department of Health and the Department of the Environment, Transport and the Regions should examine this position to see what can be done to harmonise the planning cycles and to support joint working. It is understood that the Housing Corporation has recommended moving to a three-year cycle for capital bids and this may aid joint strategy development.

2 Allocation of specific finance

Services for this client group will develop very gradually if they have to be resourced from mainstream funding. This problem will be exacerbated by the fact that the client group is concentrated in those Health Authorities which face the largest array of multiple pressures. Some of these authorities will not have had an old Victorian asylum and spend on mental health may sometimes be low relative to need. This sort of authority will find it hard to set up the necessary assertive outreach teams and other services unless they have access to extra finance.

The level of funding required is very small in relation to the NHS budget as a whole, or even the year-on-year growth monies it receives. An outreach team with 10 workers could be funded for £300-500,000 per annum and could service 100-150 clients. Given the fact that some teams already exist, it is clear that major progress could be made with only tens of millions of pounds nationally. When one takes into consideration the time required for planning, and for training and recruitment of staff, the investment levels are not unrealistic if we are serious about addressing this issue.

There are a number of ways in which specific finance could be made available, some of which have been floated before.[130] Mechanisms such as the Mental Illness Specific Grant (currently relevant only to social care), Challenge Funds, Single Regeneration Budgets, Health Action Zones and Bridging Schemes (which can allow monies to be recycled once changes have been achieved) may all be relevant. Any scheme could be independently evaluated, with further revenue dependent on the progress and outcomes demonstrable during the first few years of operation.

3 Human resources

A clear lead is needed from the centre to help establish a pool of workers who are appropriately trained and equipped to work in the type of mental health services described in this report. An agenda for action was set out in the Sainsbury Centre report *Pulling Together*.[131] This policy and implementation agenda is particularly relevant to the client group for this Review.

4 Performance management

As already stated, strong performance management of the strategic work required between local agencies will be necessary if those authorities with a weaker track record in this area are to deliver change.

One effect of the contracting and performance management culture which has existed in the NHS and elsewhere, has been a focus on short-term outputs. While this may be appropriate in some service areas it is not always helpful to the development of services for the client group for this Review. Outcomes may have to be measured using a mix of approaches and time-scales. Some national work to define measurable outcomes and indicators for the group would be helpful.

5 Other policy issues

The centre has a key role in a number of other areas of importance to the group.

▷ Public education

The client group for this Review can engender considerable public concern and sometimes even fear. This is unlikely to be dissipated until adequate services are provided, and even then occasional tragic and unavoidable incidents will occur. It is essential that staff are ready and equipped to work with the local community to inform them about services and allay their fears. Advice, support and information need to be available seven days per week if the public are to believe that services are serious about tackling crises. A greater understanding of mental health problems by the public would also be helpful and the recently increased efforts in this area are to be welcomed and need to be sustained.

▷ Uptake of benefits

Social security policy has a considerable impact on the client group. The language used in claim forms is often alienating and stigmatising. The effects of severe mental illness on a person's ability to function and work may not be well understood within the social security system. There is scope for action here both by the Department of Social Security nationally, and by staff in mental health services working constructively with Social Security local offices.

▷ The legislative framework

Some commentators have argued that this client group will only be maintained successfully in the community if Community Treatment Orders (CTOs) are introduced to give services legal powers to treat patients in the community without their consent. They argue that:

▷ there is a group of patients who currently do not comply with medication, who could be better managed if such powers were available;

▷ CTOs would be compatible with the principle of care in the least restrictive environment as they could reduce the use of compulsory inpatient stays;

▷ CTOs could be balanced by a right to receive services.

There is evidence from the United States and Australia that CTOs can be effective when adequate services, including assertive outreach teams and back-up inpatient care, are in place.

There are, however, a number of arguments against the implementation of CTOs in the UK:

▷ CTOs imply that compulsory treatment should be used prospectively to avert a breakdown; this might not be acceptable either to the UK Parliament or to the European Courts;

▷ patients might abscond or disengage to avoid compulsory medication;

▷ few staff are likely to be enthusiastic about such a measure; amongst other considerations it would not encourage mutual trust with patients, especially perhaps those from black and ethnic minorities;

▷ it might encourage bad professional practice whereby difficult patients are put on CTOs before alternatives have been explored or developed;

▷ the concept does not address the main reasons why patients deteriorate in the community – such as homelessness, poverty and lack of purposeful activity; neither does it address the reasons for non-adherence to medication.

Whilst the case for CTOs is a serious one, based partly on evidence from other countries (albeit ones where services are better developed and the institutional culture is different), the counter-arguments are also weighty. Such a step can never be an adequate substitute for proper locally based services. However, the evidence and arguments need to be kept under consideration as part of any forthcoming review of the 1983 Mental Health Act, as does evidence concerning the success of supervised discharge.

6 A national R&D strategy

Some of the findings of this report are grounded in a substantial body of research, although much of this was conducted outside the UK. Other parts of the report have had to rely more on key informants' experience, as the research base is not always strong.

Local and national implementation strategies therefore need to be underpinned by an R&D strategy to strengthen the research base. Research is required in several key areas.

▷ Social exclusion

Our current understanding of the exclusion and marginalisation process is not particularly strong. If we wish to break the cycle of social exclusion for the client group we need to identify the risk factors for becoming marginalised and the protective factors which prevent marginalisation or aid reintegration. We need to test the hypothesis that marginalisation is a temporary lifestage and that reintegration is possible under the right circumstances. Studies need to address the reasons for disengagement and the pathways back to inclusion.

▷ Needs assessment

More work is required to establish clients' views of their own needs and how best they can be supported. We also need more information about how clients sustain themselves in the community when they are unsupported. A survey of the needs of the group is required which:

▷ takes on board clients' own perceptions of their needs;

▷ describes sub-groups within this heterogeneous population;

▷ formulates an operational definition of the group;

▷ describes the long-term progress of people in this group;

▷ explores how professional practice and attitudes need to change to match need.

One of the aims should be to provide Health Authorities and other relevant agencies with a resource pack (covering methodology, procedures and instruments) that enables them to conduct their own local needs assessment. The tools provided in the pack must be piloted and standardised.

▷ Core competencies

This Review has emphasised the need for staff to engage actively with clients. Further work is required to define what makes staff competent to engage. What are the core competencies for engagement? Can these be taught or are they personality-linked? Is there an association between effectiveness, and the employment base or professional background of staff? And what is it that successful outreach workers do to maintain their effectiveness over time and to sustain their motivation and satisfaction? A framework of core competencies needs to be derived and translated into selection criteria as well as into the core elements of training programmes. The framework will also inform a set of indicators for evaluating staff performance.

▷ Alliance-building

Research is needed to clarify the key characteristics of successful networking and cooperation amongst practitioners and managers across the various agencies involved. What are the most effective, the least time-consuming and least bureaucratic methods for liaison? What is required in terms of resources, procedures and protocols to enable practitioners to develop and deliver integrated care packages?

▷ The economics of care

It would be helpful to map some real care pathways for the client group and determine to what extent services are being used appropriately relative to individual needs. More information is needed on what the total costs are. It would also be useful to examine different service configurations, including assertive outreach teams, to see which result in the most cost-effective care packages.

▷ Implementation

Studies are required to map the implementation of the assertive outreach function and elucidate the factors which facilitate or impede the implementation process.

Conclusion

We believe that this report sets out a helpful long-term strategy for developing services for the client group for this Review. This strategy is summarised in the 15 key recommendations of this Review which follow in Chapter 7. These recommendations do not encapsulate all the detailed arguments and conclusions described above, but rather attempt to identify the core actions which the various key players must take if we are to make progress and turn the vision into reality.

CHAPTER 7

The recommendations

1 Each district should set up an inter-agency strategy group to plan and monitor provision for the group

This group needs to comprise representatives of all – or as many as possible of – the key stakeholders which are listed in **Box 15** in **Chapter 6.** The group's first tasks will be:

▷ to agree operational, local definitions of the client group focusing on social disability and non-engagement;

▷ to commission a needs assessment for the district involved. This should usually be carried out by the public health department of the Health Authority working closely with social services, Trusts and primary care, which can provide local information on numbers of clients;

▷ to benchmark existing services against the basket of services required by the group, and the local needs assessment;

▷ to agree a plan, compatible with and probably forming part of local community care and mental health service plans, to develop services for, and meet the needs of, the group.

Thereafter it should monitor service development, assess changing needs and update service plans.

Lead agency: Health Authorities

2 All districts with a sufficient client-base should create one or more outreach teams to take lead responsibility for engaging with the client group

These teams should be set up and operate along the lines described in **Chapter 4.** They should consist of mental health professionals and outreach workers selected and trained to work with the client group. Such teams should integrate health and social care functions and be provided and, ideally, managed by NHS Trusts, but sometimes local circumstances will mean that teams are better provided by the independent sector. Independent sector teams will require strong links to statutory services including service level agreements with clinical staff.

Lead agencies: Health and Social Services Authorities (as commissioners), NHS Trusts and the independent sector (as providers)

3 The lead agencies should agree a set of core criteria for the selection of staff to work with the client group

The agreed selection criteria should cover personal attributes and skills which enable and support engagement (see **Chapter 4, section 4.3**).

Lead agencies: NHS Trusts, the independent sector, social care providers (hereafter, the "core service providers"), local and regional training bodies

4 Teams will require a range of expertise so that team members can act as resources for the team as a whole

When putting together a team, providers should consider the range of skills and knowledge required as well as the general competencies required of all team members. Teams should be composed of workers having a variety of training, knowledge and skills (see **Chapter 4, section 4.3**).

It will not always be possible to recruit an expert on each aspect of the care system, in which case one member within the team may wish to develop a detailed knowledge of a specific area (e.g. benefits) and function as a resource or focal point for the team as a whole.

Lead agencies: Core service providers, team leaders

5 Service providers for the client group should develop and implement training for staff

The issues which need to be covered in training are set out in **Chapter 4, section 4.3.** Training strategies must:

▷ define the key staff competencies which are required for work with the group and for which training is appropriate;

▷ put in place training mechanisms and resources to deliver the required training;

▷ link to individual staff performance appraisals and training plans;

▷ have a focus on developing understanding of the psycho-social aspects of mental health;

▷ be resourced.

Lead agencies: Core service providers

6 Managers of front-line staff must be visible and available to staff and accountable for service delivery

Staff working in services for the client group require visible management, clear leadership and regular supervision. All staff must be managerially accountable to the team leader. Specifically all staff must:

▷ have regular managerial supervision;

▷ have regular professional supervision addressing professional standards and practice;

▷ have a clear set of objectives;

▷ be aware of when and how to obtain urgent advice from line managers.

A senior manager from within each relevant provider organisation should have the oversight of services for the client group as one of his or her core priorities. The Senior Management Team of the provider agency (or equivalent) should review the state of services for the client group at least once every six months.

Lead agencies: Core service providers

7 Team members should have protected caseloads

Research and experience shows that specialist teams will not be able to deliver the best outcomes if their caseload is excessive or if the case-mix becomes diluted. Individual team members should have protected caseloads of not more than 10-15 clients (the precise numbers to be agreed locally). The upper limit on an acceptable caseload will be determined by the precise case-mix as more stable clients will require less input. Caseloads and case-mix should be reviewed regularly by management and there should be a protocol concerning discharge of clients back to the generic community mental health team or other relevant teams.

Lead agencies: Core service providers, team leaders

8 Services should make every effort to maintain contact with the families of clients

Client records should include details of close family. Family members should be contacted in order to discuss their contribution to care packages and their views should be sought wherever possible on care options and planning to prevent relapse. The client's permission should be sought to involve his or her family in the care planning process.

Lead agencies: Core service providers

9 Suitable arrangements need to be put in place for cover 24 hours per day, 7 days per week

This can be achieved in a variety of different ways. For example, a team might work on an extended hours basis (e.g. 9.00am to 9.00pm), with night-time cover provided from a residential care unit where staffing levels permit. Or alternatively, cover could be pooled, for example, between a team and a supported housing project. How exactly cover is arranged will depend on local circumstances.

Lead agencies: Health Authorities (to specify cover when commissioning), core service providers (to implement)

10 Local strategies must reflect the needs of black and ethnic minority populations

The needs of local black and ethnic minority populations must be built in at all stages including the needs assessment and strategy development. An ability to appreciate and take account of other cultures and faiths should be a key selection criterion for team members and should be further developed through training.

Lead agencies: Health Authorities, inter-agency strategy group, core service providers

11 Teams providing services for the client group should negotiate service level agreements with partner agencies

Where teams have been set up to provide services for the client group, they should work as far as possible to facilitate clients' access to ordinary or mainstream services. Service level agreements should be developed with the main partner agencies such as social services, housing, health, and independent sector agencies, which should set out what each agency can provide and what the role of the team members will be in accessing the client to each service.

Lead agency: Team leaders

12 A sufficient supply of suitable and adequately supported accommodation is required in each district

The inter-agency strategy group should set out, in its plan, the requirements for accommodation for its district. For each type of accommodation requirement a single lead agency should be agreed. The full range of accommodation options for the group will need to be considered and these are listed in **Table 1** in **Chapter 4.** However, not all districts will require this full range, as many clients will be able to live in ordinary housing with support if they receive appropriate services, and this will often be the most cost-effective solution.

Lead agencies: Health Authorities, inter-agency strategy group, Housing Authorities

13 A range of daytime activity is required in each district

As for recommendation 12, similar action is required to map the requirements for daytime activity and agree which agency is responsible for which form of provision. **Table 1** in **Chapter 4** lists the various options which may need to be available. Supported employment will for many clients be the option which they prefer and the one which is most cost-effective. Traditional forms of daycare are unlikely to be appropriate for the majority of the group. Drop-in centres, adult education and clubhouses are likely to be more acceptable.

Lead agencies: Health Authority, inter-agency strategy group

14 Clear arrangements for accessing safe 24 hour care are required

All teams must have clear arrangements for accessing safe 24 hour care, including inpatient care, where required. Teams will be responsible for accessing such care and planning discharge and should remain in contact with clients while they are in 24 hour care or hospital. This will normally be done through the psychiatrist who is part of the team.

Lead agencies: Core service providers

15 A mechanism for liaison with local child and adolescent mental health services is required to allow early intervention

Teams need to be in touch regularly with local child and adolescent mental health services as well as generic adult mental health services, to identify individuals who may benefit from early intervention.

Lead agencies: Core service providers, team leaders

References

1 The Sainsbury Centre for Mental Health (1997) *Towards Improving the Process of Acute Care.* (Unpublished).

2 The Sainsbury Centre for Mental Health (1997) *An Evaluation of the Assessment and Management of Risk.* (Unpublished).

3 Davies, L. M. & Drummond, M. F. (1994) "Economics and Schizophrenia: The Real Cost". *British Journal of Psychiatry,* 165 (Supplement 25), 18-21.

4 Davies, L. M. & Drummond, M. F. (1994) op. cit.

5 Appleby, L. (1997) *National Confidential Inquiry into Suicide and Homicide by People with Mental Illness.* Progress Report 1997. Department of Health.

6 Gath, C. & Higginson, I. (1995) *Report of the Mental Health Census. A point prevalence study. Joint project to identify people with severe and enduring mental health problems in Kensington and Chelsea and Westminster.* Department of Public Health, Kensington and Chelsea and Westminster Health Commissioning Agency.

7 Harvey, C., Pantelis, C., Taylor, J., et al. (1996) "The Camden Schizophrenia Surveys, II. High prevalence of Schizophrenia in an Inner London Borough and its relationship to socio-demographic factors". *British Journal of Psychiatry,* 168: 418 – 426.

8 King's Fund (1997) *London's Mental Health. The report to the King's Fund London Commission.* Eds. Johnson, S., Ramsay, R., Thornicroft, G., et al.

9 McCreadie, R. G. (1982) "The Nithsdale Schizophrenia Survey. I. Psychiatric and Social Handicaps". *British Journal of Psychiatry,* 140: 582 – 586.

10 Ford, R., Evans, B., Warner, L., Waller, S., Muijen, M. (1995) *Joint Health and Social Care Needs Assessment for People with Serious Mental Illness.* The Sainsbury Centre for Mental Health. (Unpublished).

11 Copsey, N. (1997) *Keeping Faith: The provision of community health services within a multi-faith context.* The Sainsbury Centre for Mental Health.

12 Scott, J. (1993) "Homelessness and Mental Illness". *The British Journal of Psychiatry,* 162: 314 – 324.

13 Menezes, P. R., Johnson, S., Thornicroft, G. et al. (1996) "Drug and Alcohol Problems among Individuals with Severe Mental Illnesses in South London". *British Journal of Psychiatry,* 168: 612 – 619.

14 Minkoff, K. & Rossi, A. (1997) *Co-Occurring Mental and Substance Disorders (Dual Diagnosis). Annotated Bibliography.* Center for Mental Health Services Managed Care Initiative: Clinical Standards and Workforce Competencies Project.

15 Drake, R. E. & Wallach, M. A. (1989) "Substance Abuse Among the Chronic Mentally Ill". *Hospital and Community Psychiatry,* 40: 1041 – 1046.

16 O'Leary, J. (1997) *Beyond help? Improving service provision for street homeless people with mental health and alcohol or drug dependency problems.* National Homeless Alliance, London.

17 Revolving Doors Agency (1996) *People with mental health problems in contact with the criminal justice system. A service mapping project in Camden and Islington.*

18 Department of Health (1996) *24 hour nursed care for people with severe and enduring mental illness.*

19 Thornicroft, G. (1991) "Social deprivation and rates of treated mental disorder. Developing statistical models to predict psychiatric service utilisation". *British Journal of Psychiatry,* 158: 475 – 484.

20 Ritchie, J., Dick, D., Lingham, R. (1994) *The Report of the Inquiry into the Care and Treatment of Christopher Clunis.* HMSO, London.

21 Rose, D. & Ford, R. (1997) *Mental Health Monitoring: CPA and Care Management Minimum Data Sets.* The Sainsbury Centre for Mental Health. (Unpublished).

22 Rose, D. & Ford, R. (1997) op. cit.

23 Jonathan Bindman, personal communication, PRiSM, Institute of Psychiatry, London.

24 Lelliott, P. and Wing, J. (1994) "A National Audit of New Long-Stay Psychiatric Patients. II: Impact on Services". *British Journal of Psychiatry,* 165: 170 – 178.

25 Lelliott, P. and Wing, J. (1994) op. cit.

26 Lelliott, P. and Wing. J. (1994) op. cit.

27 Rose, D. and Ford, R. (1997) op. cit.

28 Rose, D. (1996) *Living in the community.* The Sainsbury Centre for Mental Health.

29 Rose, D. (1996) op. cit.

30 Copsey, N. (1997) op. cit.

31 The Royal College of Psychiatrists (1996) *Report of the Confidential Inquiry into Homicides and Suicides by Mentally Ill People.*

32 Kemp, R., Hayward, P., Applethwaite, G. et al. (1996) "Compliance therapy in psychotic patients: randomised controlled trial". *British Medical Journal,* 312, 345-349.

33 Ruscher, S. M., de Wit, R., Mazmanian, D. (1997) "Psychiatric Patients' Attitudes About Medication and Factors Affecting Noncompliance". *Psychiatric Services,* 1: 82 – 85.

34 Kelly, G. R., Mamon, J. A., Scott, J. E. (1987) "Utility of the health belief model in examining medication compliance among psychiatric outpatients". *Social Science and Medicine,* 11: 1205 – 1211.

35 Leete, E. (1987) "The treatment of schizophrenia: a patient's perspective". *Hospital and Community Psychology,* 38: 486.

36 Department of Health and Home Office (1994) *Report of the Department of Health and Home Office Working Group on Psychopathic Disorder.*

37 Durrell, J., Lechtenberg, B., Corse, S., Frances, R. J. (1993) "Intensive Case Management of Persons With Chronic Mental Illness Who Abuse Substances". *Hospital and Community Psychiatry,* 44: 415 – 428.

38 Drake, R. E. & Wallach, M. A. (1989) "Substance Abuse Among the Chronic Mentally Ill". *Hospital and Community Psychiatry,* 40: 1041 – 1046.

39 Menezes, P. R., Johnson, S., Thornicroft, G., et al. (1996) op. cit.

40 Department of Health (1997) *The Spectrum of Care: Local services for People with Mental Health Problems. The Health of the Nation.*

41 Department of Health (1996) op. cit.

42 Department of Health (1990) *The Care Programme Approach for people with a mental illness referred to the specialist psychiatric services.* HC(90)23 / LASSL(90)11.

43 Department of Health (1995) *Building Bridges.* London, HMSO.

44 Department of Health (1995) *Practical Guidance on Joint Commissioning for project leaders.*

45 Department of Health (1992) *The Health of the Nation: A Strategy for Health in England.* HMSO, London.

46 Department of Health (1994) *Introduction of supervision registers for mentally ill people from 1 April 1994.* HSG(94)5.

47 Audit Commission (1994) *Finding a Place. A review of mental health services for adults.* HMSO, London.

48 Department of Health (1994) *Guidance on the discharge of mentally disordered people and their continuing care in the community.* HSG(94)27 / LASSL(94)4.

49 Department of Health (1994) op. cit.

50 Jonathan Bindman. Personal communication, PRISM, Institute of Psychiatry, London.

51 University of Manchester and Department of Health (1996) *Learning materials on mental health: Risk Assessment.* University of Manchester.

52 Department of Health (1996) *Guidance on Supervised Discharge (after-care under supervision and related provisions). Supplement to the Code of Practice published August 1993 pursuant to Section 118 of the Mental Health Act 1983.*

53 Department of Health (1997) *The New NHS.* London, HMSO.

54 NHS Executive (1996) *Review of the purchasing of mental health services by health authorities in England.*

55 The Sainsbury Centre for Mental Health (1996) *Acute Care Inpatient Study.* (Unpublished).

56 Strathdee, G. & Kendrick, T. (1996) *A General Practitioner's Guide to Good Practice in the Care of Individuals with Long-Term Mental Health Disorders.* The Maudsley Practical Handbook Series No. 4. Editors, Strathdee, G. and Phelan, M, PRiSM.

57 Hadjipateras, A., & Howard, M. (1992) *Too little … Too late. A national survey of claimants' and advisers' experiences following the introduction of Disability Living Allowance and Disability Working Allowance.* Disability Alliance / Royal Association for Disability and Rehabilitation. London.

58 Pacitti, R. & Dimmick, J. (1996) "Poverty and Mental Health: Underclaiming of Welfare Benefits". *Journal of Community and Applied Social Psychology,* 6: 395-402.

59 Lelliott, P. et al. (1996) "Mental Health Residential Care Study: Classification of Facilities and Description of Residents". *British Journal of Psychiatry,* 169: 139-47.

60 Phelan, M. & Strathdee, G. (1994) "Living in the Community: Training housing officers in mental health". *Journal of Mental Health,* 3: 229 – 233.

61 Joseph Rowntree Foundation (1997) "Housing benefit and supported housing. Findings". *Housing Research,* March.

62 Craig, T. et al. (1995) *The Homeless Mentally Ill Initiative: An evaluation of four clinical teams: Report to the Department of Health.* Department of Health.

63 NHS Executive (1996) op. cit.

64 The Sainsbury Centre for Mental Health (1996) *Acute Care Inpatient Study.* (Unpublished).

65 Muijen, M., Cooney, M., Strathdee, G., et al. (1994) "Community Psychiatric Nurse Teams: Intensive Support Versus Generic Care". *British Journal of Psychiatry,* 165: 211 – 217.

66 Marks, I. M., Connolly, J., Muijen, M., et al. (1994) "Home-based Versus Hospital-based Care for People with Severe Mental Illness". *British Journal of Psychiatry,* 165: 179 – 194.

67 Ford, R. & Ryan, P. (1997) "Labour intensive. How effective is intensive community support for people with long-standing mental illness?" *Health Service Journal,* 23 January 1997.

68 Holloway, F. & Carson, J. (1998) "Intensive case management for the severely mentally ill. Controlled Trial". *British Journal of Psychiatry,* 172: 19 – 22.

69 Marshall, M., Gray, A., Lockwood, A., et al. (1996) "Case management for people with severe mental disorders". In Schizophrenia Module of *The Cochrane Database of Systematic Reviews.* Eds. Adams, C., Anderson, J., De Jesus Mari, J. Oxford: Update Software.

70 Marks, I. M., Connolly, J., Muijen, M., et al. (1994) op. cit.

71 Ford, R. & Ryan, P. (1997) op. cit.

72 Holloway, F. & Carson, J. (1998) op. cit.

73 Ford, R., Beadsmoore, A., Ryan, P., et al. (1995) "Providing the safety net: Case management for people with a serious mental illness". *Journal of Mental Health,* 1: 91 – 97.

74 Muijen, M., Marks, I. M., Connolly, J., Audini, B. (1992) "Home based care and standard hospital care for patients with severe mental illness: a randomised controlled study". *British Medical Journal,* 304: 749 – 754.

75 Muijen et al. (1992) op. cit.

76 Beeforth, M., Conlan, E., Grayley, R. (1994) *Have we got views for you. User evaluation of case management.* The Sainsbury Centre for Mental Health.

77 Ford, R. & Ryan, P. (1997) op. cit.

78 Marks, I. M., Connolly, J., Muijen, M., et al. (1994) op. cit.

79 Scott, J. E. & Dixon, L. B. (1995) "Assertive Community Treatment and Case Management for Schizophrenia". *Schizophrenia Bulletin,* 21: 657 – 668.

80 McGrew, J. H., Bond, G. R., Dietzen, L. L. et al. (1994) "Measuring the fidelity of implementation of a mental health program model". *Journal of Consulting and Clinical Psychology,* 62: 670 – 678.

81 Stein, L I. & Test, M. A. (1980) "Alternative to mental hospital treatment: 1. A conceptual model, treatment program and clinical evaluation". *Archives of General Psychiatry,* 37: 392 – 397.

82 Hoult, J. & Reynolds, I. (1984) "Community orientated treatment compared to hospital orientated psychiatric treatment". *Social Science and Medicine,* 18: 1005 – 101.

83 Marks, I. M., Connolly, J., Muijen, M., et al. (1994) op. cit.

84 Holloway, F. & Carson, J. (1998) op. cit.

85 Gauntlett, N., Ford, R., Muijen, M. (1996) *Teamwork: Models of outreach in an urban multi-cultural setting.* The Sainsbury Centre for Mental Health.

86 Ford, R. & Ryan, P. (1997) op. cit.

87 Holloway, F. & Carson, J. (1998) op. cit.

88 Hoult, J., Reynolds, I., Charbonneau-Powis, M. et al. (1983) "Psychiatric hospital versus community treatment: the results of a randomised trial". *Australian and New Zealand Journal of Psychiatry*, 17: 160 – 167.

89 Stein, L. I. & Test, M. A. (1980) op. cit.

90 Marks, I. M., Connolly, J., Muijen, M., et al. (1994) op. cit.

91 Hoult, J. & Reynolds, I. (1984) op. cit.

92 Weisbrod, B. A., Test, M. A., Stein, L. I. (1980) "Alternative to mental hospital treatment: II. Economic benefit-cost analysis". *Archives of General Psychiatry*, 37: 392 – 397.

93 Muijen, M., Marks, I. M., Connolly, J., et al. (1992) "The Daily Living Programme. Preliminary Comparison of Community versus Hospital-Based Treatment for the Seriously Mentally Ill Facing Emergency Admission". *British Journal of Psychiatry*, 160: 379 – 384.

94 Knapp, M., Beecham, J., Koutsogeoropoulou, V., Hallam, A., et al. (1994) "Service Use and Costs of Home-Based Versus Hospital-Based Care for People with Serious Mental Illness". *British Journal of Psychiatry*, 165: 195 – 203.

95 Muijen, M., Cooney, M., Strathdee, G., et al. (1994) op. cit.

96 Marks, I. M., Connolly, J., Muijen, M., et al. (1994) op. cit.

97 Ford, R., Beadsmoore, A., Ryan, P., et al. (1995) op. cit.

98 Muijen, M., Marks, I. M., Connolly, J., et al. (1992) op. cit.

99 Bond, G. R., Miller, L. D., Krumwied, R. D., et al. (1988) "Assertive case management in three CMHCs: a controlled study". *Hospital and Community Psychiatry*, 39: 411 – 418.

100 Bond, G. R., Witheridge, T. F., Dincin, J., et al. (1990) "Assertive community treatment for frequent users of psychiatric hospitals in a large city: a controlled study". *American Journal of Community Psychology*, 18: 865 – 891.

101 Muijen, M., Cooney, M., Strathdee, G., et al. (1994) op. cit.

102 Audini, B., Marks, I. M., Lawrence, R. E., et al. (1994) "Home-based versus out-patient/in-patient care for people with serious mental illness: phase II of a controlled study". *British Journal of Psychiatry*, 165: 204 – 210.

103 Hoult, J. (1993) "Comprehensive services for the mentally ill". *Current Opinion in Psychiatry*, 6: 238 – 245.

104 McFarlane, W. R., Stastny, P., Deakins, S. (1992) "Family-aided Assertive Community Treatment: A Comprehensive Rehabilitation and Intensive Case Management Approach for Persons with Schizophrenic Disorders". In, *Effective Psychiatric Rehabilitation. New Directions for Mental Health Services No. 53*. Ed. Liberman, R. P. Jossey-Bass, San Francisco.

105 Audini, B., Marks, I. M., Lawrence, R. E., et al. (1994) op. cit.

106 Stein, L. I. & Test, M. A. (1980) op. cit.

107 Beeforth, M., Conlan, E., Grayley, R. (1994) op. cit.

108 Warner, R. (1994) *Recovery from Schizophrenia: Psychiatry and political economy*. 2nd Edition. Routledge & Kegan Paul, London.

109 Murray, A., Shepherd, G., Onyett, S., Muijen, M. (1997) *More than a friend: The role of support workers in community mental health services*. The Sainsbury Centre for Mental Health.

110 Falloon, I. R. H., Shanahan, W. J. (1990) "Community management of schizophrenia". *British Journal of Hospital Medicine*, 43: 62-66.

111 Stein, L. I. & Test, M. A. (1980) op. cit.

112 Hoult, J. & Reynolds, I. (1984).

113 McFarlane, W. R., Lukens, E., Link, B., et al. (1995) "Multiple family groups and psychoeducation in the treatment of schizophrenia". *Archives of General Psychiatry*, 52: 679 – 687.

114 Kemp, R., Hayward, P., Applethwaite, G., et al. (1996) op. cit.

115 McGorry, P. D., Edwards, J., Mihalopoulos, C., et al. (1996) "EPPIC: An Evolving System of Early Detection and Optimal Management". *Schizophrenia Bulletin*, 22: 305 – 326.

116 Chadwick, P., Birchwood, M. (1994) "The omnipotence of voices: a cognitive approach to auditory hallucinations". *British Journal of Psychiatry*, 164: 190 – 201.

117 Kingdon, D., Turkington, D., John, C. (1994) "Cognitive-behaviour therapy of schizophrenia – the amenability of delusions and hallucinations to reasoning". *British Journal of Psychiatry*, 164: 581 – 587.

118 Drake, R. E., Osher, F. C., Bartels, S. J. (1996) The "Dually Diagnosed". In *Integrated Mental Health Services*. Ed. Breakey, W. R. Oxford University Press.

119 Rose, D. & Muijen, M. (1997) "Nursing doubts". *Health Service Journal*, 26 June.

120 Mental Health Foundation (1994) *Creating Community Care*.

121 Rose, D. & Muijen, M. (1997) *24 hour nursed care for people with severe and enduring mental illness: Users' views*. The Sainsbury Centre for Mental Health.

122 Pozner, A., Ng, M. L., Hammond, J., Shepherd, G. (1997) *Working it Out. Creating work opportunities for people with mental health problems: A development handbook*. The Sainsbury Centre for Mental Health & Outset. Pavilion Publishing.

123 Dick, N. & Shepherd, G. (1995) "Work and mental health: A Preliminary test of Warr's model in sheltered workshops for the mentally ill". *Journal of Mental Health*, 3: 387 – 400.

124 All Party Parliamentary Mental Health Group (1996) *Report from the Working Group on Employment*.

125 Nehring, J., Hill, R., Poole, L. (1993) *Work, empowerment and community: Opportunities for people with long-term mental health problems: An RDP study of four new work projects*. Research and Development for Psychiatry (now the Sainsbury Centre for Mental Health).

126 Slade, M., McCrone, P., Thornicroft, G. (1995) "Uptake of welfare benefits by psychiatric patients". *Psychiatric Bulletin*, 19: 411 – 413.

127 Onyett, S., Pillinger, T., Muijen, M. (1995) *Making Community Mental Health Teams Work*. The Sainsbury Centre for Mental Health.

128 The Sainsbury Centre for Mental Health (1997) *Pulling Together. The Future Roles and Training of Mental Health Staff*.

129 NHS Confederation and The Sainsbury Centre for Mental Health (1997) *The Way Forward for Mental Health Services. A report by the NHS Confederation and The Sainsbury Centre for Mental Health*. NHS Confederation.

130 NHS Confederation and The Sainsbury Centre for Mental Health (1997) op. cit.

131 The Sainsbury Centre for Mental Health (1997) op. cit.

Appendix I
Terms of reference

The Steering Group for the Review had the following terms of reference:

▷ to advise on the values, content, and methodology of the Review and to determine what evidence and information is required to support it;

▷ to receive reports on the progress of the Review and to advise on issues which arise, including the direction of the work;

▷ to consider papers on key issues of substance relating to the Review;

▷ to comment on the draft report and advise on the related communications and dissemination strategy.

Appendix 2
Membership of the Steering Group

Dr Matt Muijen *(Chair)*
Director, The Sainsbury Centre for Mental Health

Steve Catling
Director of Mental Health Commissioning, Bromley Health Authority

David Crepaz-Keay
User consultant (and formerly President, Survivors Speak Out)

Paul Curran
Assistant Director, Commissioning & Care Management, Lewisham Social Services

Charles Fraser
Director, St Mungo's Association

Bruce Frenchum
Metropolitan Police, Community Safety & Partnership Portfolio (CO20)

Mary Hancock
The Sainsbury Centre for Mental Health (seconded from the Social Services Inspectorate, Department of Health)

Dr Frank Holloway
Consultant Psychiatrist & Clinical Director, Community Directorate, The Bethlem & Maudsley NHS Trust

Dr Andrew McCulloch
Senior Policy Adviser, The Sainsbury Centre for Mental Health

Bharat Mehta
Director, National Schizophrenia Fellowship

Rabbi Julia Neuberger
Chief Executive, King's Fund (formerly Chair, Camden & Islington Community Health Services NHS Trust)

Caroline Quest
Executive Director of Mental Affairs, Independent Healthcare Association

Professor Jan Scott
Professor of Psychiatry, University of Newcastle

Professor Geoff Shepherd
Joint Chief Executive, Health Advisory Service 2000 (formerly Head of Research, The Sainsbury Centre for Mental Health)

SECRETARIAT:

Sue Dey

Sue Parkman

Appendix 3

The call for evidence published in the *Health Service Journal* and *Community Care*

Call for evidence: Review of services for people with severe mental illness

The Sainsbury Centre for Mental Health is carrying out a Review of the policy framework and care being provided for people who are disabled by a severe mental illness, and whose problems may include:

▷ very poor social functioning;

▷ a reluctance to engage with services;

▷ problems with finding and keeping suitable accommodation;

▷ a history of dangerousness and violent behaviour;

▷ and in some cases, a secondary diagnosis of personality disorder, developmental disorder, or drug or alcohol abuse.

The Review began in November 1996 and will be completed by July 1997. It is overseen by a steering group comprising members from a range of relevant backgrounds. The purpose of the Review is to establish the nature and needs of the client group, to find out from practitioners and providers the obstacles to providing effective care and to make recommendations on the way forward.

If you are providing services for clients who you think meet these criteria, we would be very pleased to hear from you. We would be very interested to know what you provide, what approaches you think work best and what kinds of problems you have encountered in setting up and sustaining such a service.

Please contact Sue Parkman, Researcher, at The Sainsbury Centre for Mental Health, 134 - 138 Borough High Street, London SE1 1LB or Tel: 0171 403 8790, or Fax: 0171 403 9482.

Appendix 4

Participants in the focus group on black and ethnic minority mental health

FACILITATORS:

Tahera Aanchawan
(Consultant)

Yvonne Christie
(Consultant)

PARTICIPANTS:

Les Bailey
(User Group, The Sainsbury Centre for Mental Health)

Valerie Graham
(Co-ordinator, Diverse Minds, MIND)

Janice Lowe
(Executive Deputy Director, TULIP Outreach Team)

Dr David Ndegwa
(Consultant Forensic Psychiatrist & Clinical Director of Forensic Services, Lambeth Healthcare NHS Trust)

Dr Andrew McCulloch
(Senior Policy Adviser, The Sainsbury Centre for Mental Health)

Dr Matt Muijen
(Director, The Sainsbury Centre for Mental Health)

Malcolm Phillips
(Director, Ipamo)

Ganesh Sathymoorthy
(Researcher, The Sainsbury Centre for Mental Health)

Shirley Wan
(Coordinator, Chinese Mental Health Association)

SECRETARIAT:

Sue Dey

Appendix 5

Recent mental health policy

Date	Policy Initiative	Objectives relevant to this Review
1954	Run-down of the Victorian asylums begins	To resettle long-stay psychiatric patients in the community
1975	*Better Services for the Mentally Ill* White Paper	Set out the components of an integrated mental health service. Recommended hospital hostels for the new long-stay population of younger patients
1983	Mental Health Act	To provide a new framework for the compulsory admission to hospital and treatment of people with mental disorders, and protection of their human rights
1988	*The Spokes Report into the Care and Treatment of Sharon Campbell*	Recommended the establishment of a coordinated system of care for psychiatric patients and the creation of registers of patients living in the community. Stressed the importance of appropriate accommodation in sustaining aftercare arrangements
1991	*Residential needs for severely disabled psychiatric patients: The case for hospital hostels*	Recommended hospital hostels for many new long-stay patients, but identified a range of behaviour which could not be managed in these settings
1991	Introduction of the Care Programme Approach for Mentally Ill People	Laid down four main elements of care: assessment; written care plan; key worker; regular review. Aimed to ensure coordination of care
1991	*The Health of the Nation* White Paper	Set targets to reduce rates of suicide by mentally ill people Stressed that mental health services should give priority to people with the most severe illness
1992	*Mental Illness Key Area Handbook (The Health of the Nation)*	Underlined the need for 24 hour nursed care as part of the spectrum of services
1992	The Reed Review of services for mentally disordered offenders	Supported the policy that wherever possible people with mental health problems who come into contact with the criminal justice system should receive care and support from health and social services. Recommended the provision of more medium secure beds
1993	*NHS and Community Care Act 1990* came into force	Introduced the purchaser/provider split. Required health and social services to agree community care plans to meet the needs of people with enduring severe mental illness. Introduced the concept of care management

Date	Policy Initiative	Objectives relevant to this Review
1993	Guidance on the discharge of mentally ill people from hospital	Aimed to reduce risks to the public in discharge procedures, and to reinforce information systems and the care programme approach
1994	Introduction of supervision registers	Aimed to establish local registers of people with severe and enduring mental illness thought to be at risk of suicide, serious violence to others, or severe self-neglect
1994	*Mental Illness Key Area Handbook* (second edition)	Stressed that services should be targeted on people with severe mental illness and made suggestions about assessing high, medium and low support needs
1995	*Building Bridges: A guide to arrangements for inter-agency working for the care and protection of severely mentally ill people*	Aimed to draw together lessons about collaborative working and to increase coordination of services
1996	Introduction of supervised discharge	Provides a form of guardianship for use by health professionals with detained patients whose aftercare may break down
1996	*The Spectrum of Care*	Stressed the need for 24 hour nursed care, crisis services and intensive home support as part of a range of provision
1996	*24 hour nursed care for people with severe and enduring mental illness*	Recommended that the development of 24 hour nursed care should be given priority and suggested an action plan

Appendix 6

Key elements of the assertive outreach approach

Derived from Teague, G. B. (1996) *Assertive Community Treatment (ACT) Implementation Measures & Analyses.* Unpublished paper. Bethesda, July 12.

Figures given are for guidance only.

1 Human resources

▷ Small caseload (client : team member ratio of 10-15:1)

▷ Regular review of care plan for each client

▷ Team leader is a practitioner with a caseload

▷ Continuity of staffing

▷ Psychiatrist on staff (client : psychiatrist ratio of 100:1)

▷ Nurse on staff

▷ Substance abuse specialist on staff (client : team member with substance abuse training / experience ratio of 50:1)

▷ Employment rehabilitation specialist on staff (client : team member with employment rehabilitation training / experience ratio of 100:1)

▷ Team consists of at least 10 staff

2 Organisational boundaries

▷ Explicit admission criteria

▷ Intake rate of 6 clients per month or fewer

▷ Full responsibility for treatment services

▷ Responsibility for crisis services / 24 hour cover

▷ Responsibility for hospital admissions

▷ Responsibility for hospital discharge planning

▷ Service not limited to specific time periods

3 Nature of services

▷ Team members work in the community in the clients' own settings

▷ Clients do not drop out but are maintained at a satisfactory level of engagement

▷ Assertive engagement mechanisms including street outreach

▷ Service is as intense as required

▷ Service contacts are as frequent as required

▷ Services work with families and with clients' own support systems

Appendix 7
Costings for six care packages

Option 1: Whole year in 24 hour nursed care

	wks	£pw[1]	NL	London[2]
24 hour nursed care[3]	52	693.19	36,046	43,976
Total (97/8)			**36,046**	**43,976**

(1) Unit costs / weekly costs are for non-London, uprated to 97/98 prices using GDP deflator.

(2) Unit costs for London services adjusted by 1.22 multiplier to reflect higher costs of provision.

(3) *24 hour nursed care for people with severe and enduring mental illness,* Department of Health, 1996.

Option 2: Whole year in DISH, but with 3 weeks in acute in-patient care

	wks	£pw[4]	NL	London[5]
DISH[6]	52	237.62	12,356	15,075
+ Council flat[7]	52	35.14	1,827	2,229
Other day services[8]	52	59.08	3,072	3,748
3 weeks in-patient care[9]				
Non-London	3	850	2,551	
London	3	1,076		3,227
Total (97/8) excl. other day services			**16,734**	**20,531**
Total (97/8) incl. other day services			**19,807**	**24,279**

(4) All unit costs / weekly costs uprated to 97/98 prices using GDP deflator.

(5) Unit costs for London services adjusted by 1.22 multiplier to reflect higher costs of provision, when not provided by source data.

(6) Derived from Nottingham Rehabilitation & Community Care Services, Nottingham Healthcare Trust (DISH Accounts) 1997

(7) Rental figure relates to average local authority relets of one-bedroom flats, non-London. London rent £42. If property is a Housing Association relet the average weekly rent would be £45 non-London and £50 London. Estimates from *Housing Today,* National Housing Federation, 29/5/97; and *NHF Core Bulletin* April-June 1997.

(8) Chisholm, D. et al. (1997), "The Costs of Mental Health Residential Care", *Journal of Mental Health,* 6,1:85-89, derived from *Table 3: Mean weekly hospital and community service use costs by residential setting.* **Note:** usage of other day services, such as day centres, varies according to type of accommodation and attached support provided. Living in own council flat assumed to use other day services equivalent to people in group homes. This may be an underestimate.

(9) Chisholm, D., *ibid.*

NOTE: Costings do not include social security benefits, except Housing Benefit.

NL = Non London

Option 3: Whole year in community (council flat) with assertive outreach, but with 6 weeks in acute in-patient care

	wks	£pw[10]	NL	London[11]
52 weeks council flat[12]	52	35.14	1,827	2,229
Assertive outreach[13]	52	39.96	2,078	2,535
Other day services[14]	52	59.08	3,072	3,748

96/7(additional £2,792 per year (58.71 per wk) assuming person attends day centre)

6 weeks in-patient[15]				
Non-London	6	850.3	4,638	
London	6	1075.8		5,868
Total (97/8) excl. other day services			**8,543**	**10,633**
Total (97/8) incl. other day services			**11,616**	**14,381**

(10) All unit costs / weekly costs uprated to 97/98 prices using GDP deflator.

(11) Unit costs for London services adjusted by 1.22 multiplier to reflect higher costs of provision, when not provided by source data.

(12) See footnote (7).

(13) Estimates from Elmore Committee Oxford, Annual Report 1996, based on total expenditure divided by number of referrals.

(14) Chisholm op.cit., see footnote (8).

(15) Chisholm, ibid.

Option 4: 'Peter' (a simplification of a real case history): 1 month in acute in-patient care, 2 months in low support hostel with CMHT support, 1 month in acute in-patient care, 2 weeks in community (B&B), Arrested. Court Diversion scheme in operation so 6 weeks in acute in-patient care, 2 weeks in B&B, 2 weeks homeless, 1 month in acute in-patient care, arrested after discharge, rest of the year in prison.

	wks	£pw[16]	NL	London[17]
18 weeks in-patient[18]				
Non-London	18	850.3	15,305	
London	18	1075.8		19,364
8 weeks low support hostel[18]				
Non-London	8	277	2,218	
London	8	323		2,587
Other day services[19]	8	40	324	389
CMHT involvement[20]	8	99	791	949
4 weeks B&B[21]	4	93	360	432
other day services[19]	4	40	162	194
2 weeks homeless[22]				
Non-London	2	273	546	
London	2	323		647
Other day services[19]	2	40	81	99
20 weeks prison[23]	20	412	8,230	9,877
Total (97/8) excl. other day services			27,450	33,856
Total (97/8) incl. other day services			28,017	34,538

(16) All unit costs / weekly costs uprated to 97/98 prices using GDP deflator.

(17) Unit costs for London services adjusted by 1.22 multiplier to reflect higher costs of provision, when not provided by source data.

(18) Chisholm, *op.cit.*

(19) Chisholm, ibid. Use of other day services such as day centres has been included.

(20) Netten, A. and Dennett J., *Unit Costs of Health and Social Care,* PSSRU, 1997 p36. Two hours per week CMHT direct patient contact assumed.

(21) Carter, M., (1997) *The Last Resort: living in B&B in the 1990s,* Shelter, London. Weekly charges for single person in B&B varies from £29.44 to £168 per week. Carter suggests a non-London (median) rate of £55 per week which has been used here.

(22) Assumes stays in homeless hostel equivalent to low staffed hostel, Chisholm, *op cit.*

(23) *Prison Service Annual Report and Accounts* April 94/5, uprated to 97/8 prices.

Option 5: **2 months in hospital in-patient care, 2 months in B&B with CMHT support, 1 month in hospital, 3 months in B&B with CMHT support, 1 month in hospital, rest of the year in a medium support hostel with CMHT support**

	Weeks	£pw[24]	NL	London[25]
16 weeks in-patient[26]				
Non-London	16	850.3	13,605	
London	16	1075.8		17,213
20 weeks B&B[27]	20	92.7	1,854	2,262
CMHT support[28]	20	98.88	1,978	2,413
Other day services[29]	20	40.48	810	988
16 weeks medium support hostel[26]				
Non-London	16	274	4,382	
London	16	446		7,141
With CMHT support[28]	16	98.88	1,582	1,930
Other day services[29]	16	49.49	792	966
Total (97/8) excl. other day services			**23,401**	**30,959**
Total (97/8) incl. other day services			**25,002**	**31,946**

(24) All unit costs / weekly costs uprated to 97/98 prices using GDP deflator.

(25) Unit costs for London services adjusted by 1.22 multiplier to reflect higher costs of provision, when not provided by source data.

(26) Chisholm, *op cit.*

(27) Carter, M., *op cit.* See footnote (21).

(28) Netten, A., *op cit.* Two hours per week CMHT direct patient contact assumed.

(29) Chisholm, *op cit.* Use of other day services such as day centres has been included.

Option 6: **3 months in acute in-patient care, 5 months in own accommodation with 2 out-patient appointments, 2 months in acute in-patient care, 2 months in own accommodation with 2 out-patient appointments.**

	Weeks	£pw[30]	NL	London[31]
22 weeks in-patient[32]				
Non-London	16	850	13,605	
London	16	1,076		17,213
30 weeks own accommodation				
Private rented[33]	30	51	1,535	1,872
Other day services[34]	30	59	1,772	2,162
4 out-patient appointments[35]	4	95	378	462
Total (97/8) excl. other day services			**15,518**	**19,547**
Total (97/8) incl. other day services			**17,290**	**21,709**

(30) All unit costs / weekly costs uprated to 97/98 prices using GDP deflator.

(31) Unit costs for London services adjusted by 1.22 multiplier to reflect higher costs of provision, when not provided by source data.

(32) Chisholm, *op.cit.*

(33) *Housing Today, op cit.,* own accommodation assumed to be private rented.

(34) Chisholm, *op cit.* Use of other day services such as day centres has been included.

(35) Netten, A., *op cit.*